Kenilworth (

# Kenilworth Chapter

Leonard Unsworth

YOUCAXTON PUBLICATIONS

OXFORD & SHREWSBURY

Printed and bound in Great Britain.
Published by Leonard Unsworth
YouCaxton Publications

ISBN 978-191117-533-9

# Contents

# Preface

After recounting some of his own educational experiences in a book entitled *Educating Kenilworth*, the author had numerous requests for a sequel. 'What happened next?' everybody wanted to know. Well leather up! Here's your invitation to join this *Kenilworth Chapter* for a few hours.

In 1967, Lenny reached the age of fifteen, making him old enough to legally depart the educational system, which he was invited to do. Without any qualifications or help, save orders from Dad to get a job, prospects of meaningful employment did not look great, and at home the complex relationship between father and son during this socially challenging period made it hard for them relate to each another. With his dreams of riding a motorbike constantly being denied, Lenny embarked on a capricious journey, not without consequence, towards manhood. No master plan, just self-reliance, youthful enthusiasm, friendships along the way and a carefree sense of invincibility.

# Get a Job

Shattered and sundered by his plight, Lenny trudged the streets of his hometown without direction, orders from Dad ringing in his ears. 'Get a job – a real one – not a paper round; and if you can't do that, get out.'

Kenilworth was not exactly a hotbed of employment or opportunity in 1967, especially for a fifteen-year-old without qualifications, so things did not look great. Where could he go for work? What work could he do? Who could he turn to for help?

Eventually Lenny called on his best mate, Timmy, only to be told he wasn't welcome anymore as Timmy's Mum thought Lenny was a bad influence on her son. This only compounded Lenny's woes and he now stood very alone. Even a visit to the youth club was ruled out as it was closed for the Easter break. Then, quite by chance, Lenny bumped into Mr West, the curate of Saint Nicholas Church, who asked him what he had been up to and told him that if he was at a loose end he should visit the boys' club. The fact that Lenny was no longer a member of the club and didn't sing in the church choir anymore seemed not to bother Mr West, who assured Lenny he would be very welcome, which was great news, for some socialising was exactly the required medicine.

The following evening, Lenny returned to his old stomping ground of Saint Nicholas Boys' Club, which was sited in the gardens at the rear of Kenilworth Parochial Church Hall. The boys' club had originally been built to aid injured soldiers of the First World War and clues to its former use were evident on entry in the form of a ramp, which would have assisted wheelchair access. Inside there were shutters, which opened wide to maximise airflow and helped the breathing of victims of gas. The other climatic control feature was a cylindrical coke-burning stove, providing warmth and comfort during the colder months for those convalescing soldiers of The Great War.

*Pic 1, St Nicholas Boys Club.*

*Pic 2, Shutters, visible inside the club.*

Putting on a brave face to re-enter the club turned out to be unnecessary as a warm welcome was afforded, not least from the roaring stove, and before long it felt like he'd never been away. Most popular of the indoor activities for club-goers was table tennis and Lenny soon got to grips with his old skills and was smashing ping-pong balls about.

Later that evening, during snack time, Lenny got chatting with an old football teammate, Brian Bachelor – nickname Hog. Not sure why he was called Hog, but Hog it was. Hog was one school year older than Lenny and had joined the Navy. To earn some extra cash before his posting date, he had taken up employment at a department store and, as he would be leaving soon, his job would become vacant.

Lenny wasn't interested in joining the forces – for that meant haircuts, which were not Lenny's style – but what Hog had to say about his employment at the department store made Lenny's ears prick up. Hog explained that he was working on maintenance at the largest department store in Leamington Spa, Burgis and Colbourne, and would be leaving soon, so his post would become vacant. If Lenny was interested in the job, he should pen a letter to head of personnel, Mrs Whitehouse, who just happened to live in Kenilworth. Hog would supply her details.

This felt good – a sudden note of optimism appearing quite out of the blue. It lifted Lenny and he was eager to get his sister Jean on board to help compose a letter of application, which she agreed so to do. When the draft was finished, Lenny carefully copied it out, taking care not to make any mistakes – he really wanted this to be good – before popping it in the postbox, fingers crossed.

§

Meanwhile, life continued with early starts for Lenny – he had to be at the paper shop in Whitemoor Road by six each morning, getting the papers marked up ready for delivery. On return home, he took care of his little sister, Julie, delivering her safely to and from the nursery in Bertie Road. During the day, Lenny often entertained himself with his airgun, taking it all to pieces then reassembling it before taking potshots at things he shouldn't.

One day while waiting for news of the job, Dad left Lenny a couple of shillings with instructions to go down the gasworks for a bucket of creosote to do the shed – gasworks extracted flammable gas from coal and were noted for belching out foul-smelling smoke; creosote was a by-product of the process and was used as a wood preservative. Instead of following Dad's instructions to preserve the shed, Lenny set about destroying it, using the door for target practice to sight up his gun, which split the wood and filled it with lead.

When Dad returned home that evening, he spotted Lenny's handiwork and finally lost his temper. He ran inside the house attacking Lenny with both fists and flaying him. Lenny managed to parry off this onslaught and slip out the house until things calmed down, but their relationship was now at an all-time low with something needing to change quick.

§

The following day a sudden shock united the whole family in grief. Blackie, the family pet poodle, had got out and been struck by a van. Dad retrieved Blackie's lifeless blood-soaked carcass from the road and carried it down the drive to the back garden, laying it on the lawn. Dad prepared a grave with his spade to a depth of about three feet and placed Blackie in. He was just about to backfill when Lenny thought he saw Blackie blink. This was just enough to convince Dad to lift him back out and place him in his basket for further examination. It turned out to be true. Blackie *had* blinked and after a couple of weeks convalescing made a full recovery. Miraculously he had risen from the grave.

*Pic 3, Blackie.*

Curiously, Blackie's accident melted the ice somewhat between father and son, also helped by the arrival of an important letter addressed to Lenny, who couldn't have been more excited to tear open the envelope. Instantly he spotted the headed notepaper of Burgis and Colbourne. It was a reply to his application, inviting him to attend an interview for a job on maintenance at the department store in Leamington Spa.

Lenny thought this was great, and it also ignited family enthusiasm to help in any way they could. Short of putting in a decent appearance, old school tie included, his most pressing problem was how he would cope with the twelve-mile tour to Leamington and back, but only the excursion itself would answer that.

The big day came soon enough, and Lenny trialled his bike on the six-mile course to Burgis and Colbourne. Presenting himself at the rear of the store in the delivery bay, Lenny was met by the foreman of maintenance, who introduced himself as Albert. He was a little man wearing a brown cow-gown – which fitted him down to the ground – and who jangled wherever he went as he was the proud keeper of the keys.

Albert told Lenny he was going to show him around the store before his interview at the manager's office. Although not realising it at the time, Lenny was being closely monitored by Albert, who would have the final say as to who got the job.

Descending together in the goods lift, which juddered to a halt as it reached the basement, Albert and Lenny began the tour. Albert said that Lenny was the third and final interviewee of the day as he showed him around. Albert pointed out various areas of the basement, including services, storage, fridges and freezers before moving on to a stairwell to climb, emerging on the ground floor. To the rear of the store was a quality food hall, with the front of the store supporting various retail outlets. Alongside the stairwell, also giving access to the upper floors, was the customer lift, which was permanently manned. The operator was a large man, also wearing a brown cow-gown. He only had one arm, but this didn't seem to impede him in any way and was a great attraction to all the kids.

The final stages of the tour took in the top floor where there was a works canteen, a cash office and the manager's office where Lenny would attend his interview.

Albert knocked on the door and walked straight in, with Lenny having been invited to wait outside until called. After a minute or so, the call came and Lenny entered the office to take a seat in front of a large oak desk. Sat behind the desk was a lady, who introduced herself as the manager, and who wore the bluest of rinses. She went through a few of the basics, but seemed impressed with Lenny's application letter along with his work record of marking up and delivering the papers each morning. Not fifteen minutes had passed when the interview concluded and Lenny was escorted to the canteen and given a cup of tea with instructions to wait until Albert got back to him. He had just got down to the tea leaves when Albert returned with some startling news: Lenny had been invited to return to the manager's office. Heart racing, he wondered what it was all about. Upon entry Lenny was told he had been selected for the job on maintenance, which, if he accepted, could start the following Monday with an expected weekly wage of four pound ten shillings. Lenny thought this was great and eagerly agreed on the terms.

This life-changing event propelled Lenny home in lightning quick time – he couldn't wait to get back to announce the good news. His worries about the twelve-mile bike ride seemed to have evaporated, at least for now. Back home, although Dad was not visibly thrilled with Lenny's success, he did at least give some credit to the achievement. This didn't seem to bother Lenny, who was full of plans for the future: things he could buy and save for. The first reality check came from Dad, via Mum, informing Lenny that as of his first wage he would be expected to pay board of one pound ten shillings a week. Lenny moaned a bit, but thought it was okay because it still left three pounds a week to play with.

Plans started to take shape in preparation for the big day: Mum was going to make sandwiches for Lenny; his saddlebag needed a bike spanner and puncture repair kit; and he needed to get a cape, in case of rain. Lenny wanted to wear his jeans, but Dad thought it more appropriate to wear his old school trousers.

# First Day

When that first day of work dawned, Lenny set off at 7.30am – passing his old school and heading down Rocky Lane towards Leamington – to set him in good time to arrive for 8.15am, which he did, taking care to securely lock up his bike. Reporting for duty, Lenny was met by Albert, who issued him with his very own cow-gown along with instructions that he would be working close to Albert during his training period until he got to know the ropes.

That first day, Lenny shadowed Albert, lifting boxes and delivering them to various locations using a sack truck. It was fun getting to know the full layout of the store, visiting all departments and meeting his new work colleagues. When it was time for a break, it was up to the canteen for a cup of tea and a KitKat. You could take your sandwiches up there for lunch too if you wanted, or go out of the store, being sure not to be back late.

After lunch, a complete tour of the store was required to retrieve all empty boxes, along with packaging, and take them down to the loading bay where they had to be flattened, compressed by a machine and tied with string into bales ready for collection. To the rear of the store, on the ground floor level, was a quality food hall, which had to be continuously supplied with fresh produce from around the globe, so things could get very busy.

Five o'clock arrived, which signalled time to shut shop and lock the doors. This could take up to thirty minutes because it was very important to make sure everybody was out of the store.

As far as Lenny was concerned though, it was time to unlock his bike and pedal home along the busy Kenilworth Road, which could be quite dangerous for cyclists. It wasn't until he got into the leafy lanes that he felt able to relax and reflect on what he thought had been a very positive first day.

Mum didn't know quite what time Lenny would be home for his tea, so it was cold by the time he arrived and needed reheating in the oven. As Lenny sat down at the table, the family gathered around to hear about his first day, which was recounted in great detail.

It took a couple of weeks to settle into the new routine, but it didn't take Dad that long before he was coming out with negative comments about the job. 'There's no skill in it,' he would say. 'No prospects. You can't play football anymore working Saturdays. You're no more than a labourer.' This didn't matter that much to Lenny, who hadn't been playing much football lately anyway and was happy in his new job, but it hadn't gone unnoticed that working Saturdays excluded him from the game he loved, and he was also mindfully aware of the twelve-mile cycle ride.

§

The road Lenny cycled to and from work took him past his old school and along Rocky Lane, skirting the tiny village of Ashow, known locally as the Pepper Mines. It was there that Lenny's friend, Gordon Fortnum, lived in a cottage with his mother. Gordon wasn't much of a footballer, but Lenny remembered training him up to play right back in the school's cup-winning side. Occasionally, the pair would bump into each other and chat about their shared interests – top of the list being motorbikes. Gordon was studying hard at school hoping to get some O-levels, so he could take up an apprenticeship. Meanwhile, he had got himself a Saturday job at Jack Butler's motorbike shop in Leamington. The shop was close to where Lenny worked, so the pair decided to cycle in together on Saturdays. Gordon told Lenny that he'd got hold of an old 125cc BSA Bantam motorbike, and if he wanted to come down to the cottage he could have a look at it. Sunday was a good day, as it was Lenny's day off, so he arranged to call.

Although not roadworthy, the motorbike did have wheels, a saddle and an engine, which if kicked over often enough would start up intermittently. It felt great to sit astride, twist the throttle and imagine taking off into the distance. As the Bantam wasn't running well, Gordon was constantly cleaning the spark plug, but this didn't seem to help. However, with Lenny's assistance, he removed a cover plate from the side of the crankcase and discovered that the contact breakers needed gapping. Once fixed everything jumped into gear.

At the rear of Gordon's cottage was a rough piece of ground, which could be circumnavigated. Lenny had boasted to Gordon about his motorbike ability despite the fact that he had never ridden one before. The boys thought one of the most important skills was letting out the clutch without stalling the engine, so when the moment arrived for Lenny's first clutch drop, he was determined not to stall. He throttled back hard, dropped the clutch and shot the old village bike forward, nearly wrenching his arms from his sockets, but the lad held on and completed the course absolutely exhilarated.

Having now acquired the feel, along with some basic skills, Lenny and Gordon thought it would be good to ride around a bigger track. So the lads pushed the bike up the lane to the top field where they circled time and time again until the tank ran dry and the bike spluttered to a halt.

Gordon's motorbike became widely talked about, and it wasn't long before a group of lads descended on the Pepper Mines for trials. All intoxicated by the experience vowed to form a Kenilworth chapter and get motorbikes as soon as they could. For the moment though, Lenny was stuck with his pushbike.

§

Lenny's route home from work took him up Common Lane, one of the steepest hills in Kenilworth, and past his best mate's house, which was about halfway up. Timmy and Lenny had been banned from seeing each other by Timmy's mother, so when Lenny got halfway up the hill he would feign exhaustion and dismount his bike, slowly pushing it past Timmy's house. Timmy knew roughly what time to expect Lenny, so he would hang about in the garden ready for their secret rendezvous.

Timmy's dad had recently taken over a new warehouse, built on land at the back of Lenny's house, and it was there the lads liked to meet up when the workers had gone home. It was a good place to hang out, with a wall to kick a ball against. It felt strange for Lenny to be socialising with his old friends, who were still at school, as his new life was one of work and wages, but they were all interested in what Lenny was doing, and how he was getting on, and Lenny was always pleased to see them.

On Saturdays, Lenny looked forward to his lunch break when he would pop over to Jack Butler's to see Gordon. The two lads would look over the motorbikes and chat about the technical data. During the week, Lenny would spend his lunch break either in the staff canteen or looking around the shops on the Parade. Now earning a weekly wage, the attraction of being able to afford a pair of Beatle boots became too much, so Lenny splashed out £7 – which was nearly two week's wages – and purchased a pair. Lenny thought they were worth every penny and at break time a girl named Elizabeth commented on them. She was seventeen and had worked at the store in Haberdashery for about a year, and she wondered if Lenny was interested in going to the pictures to see the latest film. Lenny *was* interested but worried about returning home late in the dark as his bike didn't have any lights, so he declined the offer. Liz was keen though and came up with another idea – she suggested that she come over to Kenilworth on the bus. Lenny said he didn't think there was much they could do as he wouldn't be able to take her to his house, but Liz said not to worry, 'We can go for a walk. All you need is love.' So it was arranged to meet at the bus stop at seven that evening.

Lenny was excited about his date, so got to the bus stop early to be sure not to miss Liz. She arrived as arranged and looked great, wearing fashion clothes and makeup that she didn't wear to work. It was a lovely evening and the couple set off for a walk along the bridleway, hand in hand. After about thirty minutes they returned, coming back alongside Timmy's dad's warehouse where there was a side door that only needed a bump to open. Lenny explained that it was okay to go in as he often frequented the building and it belonged to his best mate's dad.

Once inside, they went through to the front office, which was kitted out with an old sofa, down the side of which was a secret stash of sweet cider belonging to the lads. Liz and Lenny nestled down and glugged some cider and Liz pulled out a packet of ten cigarettes. Lenny wasn't interested in smoking, but Liz was keen to show off her skills – first she demonstrated inhaling, then exhaling from both nostrils, leaving lipstick on the filter, and following up with smoke rings. Eventually she put the packet of ten back in her handbag and pulled out a packet of three. Lenny hadn't seen this brand before, but Liz was an expert with zips, what with working in haberdashery, so Lenny raised no objections to receiving a full demonstration. The date concluded with a few more glugs of cider, then back to the bus stop for Liz to catch her bus.

# Battered Sausage

Lenny's older sister Jean had got herself a boyfriend from Finham in Coventry named Sam Hunt. He was a rocker and Dad did not approve, so Sam would ride his motorbike over to Kenilworth to meet secretly with Jean on Dalehouse Lane. Like any annoying little brother, Lenny would often tag along – he was in awe of Sam's 150cc Francis Barnet motorbike, which was bright red in colour – being ex-GPO – and had been used for delivering telegrams. Lenny thought Sam looked great with his black leather jacket and blonde flowing hair and would pester him into giving pillion rides. One evening, about two weeks after Sam and Jean had started going out, Sam said he was going to be getting another motorbike, along with a new set of leathers, so if Lenny wanted his old leather jacket he could have it.

The next time Lenny saw Sam, the rocker was sitting astride a brand new 650cc Triumph Bonneville wearing a new leather jacket. As promised, he gave Lenny his old jacket, telling him it only needed a bit of stitching in the lining and then would be better than new, as it was already broken in. Lenny slipped it on and zipped it up, grinning. Then Sam patted the saddle of his new bike to indicate that Lenny should get on. He told Lenny he'd take him for a spin, but that he wouldn't be doing the ton that evening as the bike was not yet run in. Sam said he could, however, demonstrate the terrific acceleration of his new machine, which turned out to be an unimaginable experience and left Lenny even more desperate to own one himself.

But what to do with the leather jacket? Lenny could expect big trouble if Dad found it – there would be no rockers in *his* house – so Lenny packed it away in a little blue suitcase under his bed and smuggled it out each time he wanted to wear it.

§

A few days later, on the way home from work, Lenny 'bumped' into Timmy on Common Lane and learnt the news that he was having a party – a camp-over in his back garden. Timmy said he would work on his mum to see if she would give permission for Lenny to attend and, to everyone's surprise, permission was granted. The camp-over was a great success and Lenny was back in the good books. The two lads couldn't have been more excited. Now they could meet openly and with Lenny's new spending power could easily afford double portions of chips.

It was one evening, walking back from the chip shop, that Timmy told Lenny he had heard some hot news – the police had been called to Kenilworth School on Leyes Lane to investigate a case of spray can graffiti, which was rocking the establishment. The lads were quick to get down there to have a good look. The graffiti, which could clearly be seen from the road, read, "Pot is Peace" – an extraordinary thing to appear in the small conservative town of Kenilworth in those days. Lenny thought he knew who had the balls to do it because it carried the tag of an old 'Pal' of his from way back. Timmy quipped, "Pot is *Police*" as they walked away with their chips. The incident highlighted that social norms were changing rapidly, and every time Lenny passed the graffiti on his way to work, he couldn't help but smile.

§

As Dad predicted, working Saturdays did present some difficult choices. Lenny's favourite football team was Coventry City FC, and he had been going to Highfield Road regularly since before Jimmy Hill took them to the top. When Lenny's mates told him they were planning a visit to the ground one Saturday and asked if he wanted to join them, he was disappointed to have to decline. Another time, Timmy wanted Lenny to go with him to the Saturday afternoon matinee, which was showing a Fistful of Dollars – a spaghetti western starring Clint Eastwood – but again it was a Saturday no show.

There was one Saturday show, however, that Lenny was not about to miss. So when an old school friend, Linda, penned him a note inviting him to accompany her to the old Priory Theatre on Rosemary Hill, Lenny agreed on one condition: that he was back in time for Match of The Day.

Lenny liked a bit of theatre and the couple enjoyed the production, sitting at the back of the auditorium holding hands. After the curtain call, they were first through the exit and down the road to the School Lane chippie to avoid the queue and any delay getting back for Lenny's favourite show. While they were waiting to be served, Linda explained she was house-sitting for a family who had gone away for the weekend, and it would be okay to go back to the house to watch the match. The two theatregoers arrived just in time to get comfortable on the sofa for the programme. During a lull in the action, Lenny asked Linda whose house it was.

'Jimmy Hill's,' she replied, 'the Coventry City manager.'

So there Lenny was, on Jim's sofa, enjoying his battered sausage and watching Match of the Day.

# Hard Peas

Finding some perks while enjoying his work often took Lenny down to the freezer room where there was usually an open box of raspberry ripple ice cream tubs. He'd learnt to slip one in his cow-gown pocket, then disappear to enjoy it in the privacy of the toilet cubicle.

One day, Lenny went down to the freezer room to help himself, but there was a sack of frozen peas stacked on top of the ice cream box that needed moving to gain access to the ice creams. The sack was moved and an ice cream disappeared, but when Lenny dropped the sack of peas back into place, it burst open, spewing its contents far and wide, completely covering the freezer room floor with frozen peas. Thinking on his toes, Lenny disappeared to consume the evidence, which would have connected him to the scene of the crime. An enquiry was set up and, racked with guilt, Lenny confessed to his foreman what had happened but not why. Albert told him to *'worry not'*; he would clear the matter up.

Albert liked Lenny, so he was quite protective towards the lad, and the two of them were developing a good relationship; Dad was less than happy with this, though, and thought Albert to be a negative influence on his son, who now seemed to be short on ambition.

On the night of the pea incident, Dad had another pop at Lenny, saying the job at Burgis and Colbourne required no skill and was heading nowhere: Lenny should be looking to get himself a trade – and if he still thought he was going to be a footballer, he should forget it because no team would want him. Lenny thought he had been doing quite well, but Dad's rant resonated. Nevertheless, he ignored it for the moment – this adolescent boy was enjoying himself and saving his wages towards a secret agenda.

§

A few days later, Dad brought a pile of papers home for Lenny to look at. The papers turned out to be an application form for an apprenticeship at an engineering company called Automotive Products or Lockheed Brakes. The company was second to none, according to Dad, and one of the highest-paid engineering firms in the country. It attracted a workforce of over five thousand from far and wide and boasted the finest training and sports facilities. The firm selected only the cream from the top, priding itself on its apprenticeship schemes, and even providing hostel accommodation for those who didn't live locally.

Dad asked Lenny what he thought about doing an apprenticeship, to which Lenny replied he might fancy being a bricklayer. This was not the answer Dad was looking for and went on at great length to explain that bricklaying was open to the effects of climatic conditions, including winter, whereas a skilled job in engineering was not. He also pointed out that, while training, an apprentice could expect a weekly wage and to be released for college to gain valuable qualifications. But it was difficult for Dad to paper over the fact that Lenny would be indentured for five years.

Lenny thought this was all pie in the sky – to gain an apprenticeship required a minimum of Maths and English qualifications, and for that you needed to complete a fifth year at school or college. In any case, a company like Lockheed would look for grammar school lads. Not much hope there then. Nevertheless, Dad said the application form was worth considering for the future. Lenny wasn't so sure: he did not see himself back at school or college gaining the necessary qualifications. But before Dad put the papers away, he spotted a remarkable coincidence – the intake date for that year was September 4th: applicants had to be sixteen on or before this date. September 4th also just happened to be Lenny's birthday, qualifying him to apply by a matter of hours. Dad thought that for no other reason than this – that Lenny was eligible to apply – that he *should* apply, not least because it would be good experience. With some more persuasion, Dad won Lenny over and the boy agreed to give it a go. Lenny did not, however, hold out much hope for success.

After some delay on Lenny's part – there were always more interesting things to do – Dad told him to get a move on. The forms needed to be submitted in good time and would also require a reference from Lenny's current employer. Dad's advice was to not tell anybody at work that he was applying for the apprenticeship, but just to say that he needed a reference to attend night school. Dad found several mistakes when he checked through Lenny's application forms, but his tip to fill them out in pencil first meant mistakes could easily be rectified. Lenny's pile of papers grew ready for presentation, with his school report hidden right at the bottom. For now just the application forms were required though, and were to be sent off by first-class post in a big brown envelope to the Lockheed.

If there was to be even an outside chance of success at interview, Dad thought it was worth brushing up on some basics – Lenny had always been okay with numbers, but the same could not be said for literacy. More worrying for Dad was his lad's attitude: Lenny showed little enthusiasm, and this needed addressing too, so Dad devised a plan. There was to be a charity football match, which would be held under floodlights at the Windmill Ground, home of Lockheed FC, Leamington's top football team, and Dad's friend was the secretary of the club and was organising the event. He had let Dad know that there might be some professional footballers turning out on the night and if Lenny fancied a kick around the boy should bring his boots. That did the trick! Lenny was full of it and couldn't have been more excited at the prospect of playing at the Windmill under lights.

§

On the evening of the match, Dad and Lenny arrived early to get a parking space for Dad's VW Beetle in the Windmill car park. With time to spare before kick off, Dad took Lenny over to the sports and social club belonging to Lockheed Brakes, which just happened to be across the road. There was a wonderful pitch alongside the clubhouse, with a match in progress, and another pitch further down, by some fantastic changing rooms. Lenny had never seen facilities like this before – he was used to park pitches – and the idea of joining Lockheed as an apprentice started to appeal. Then the father and son went back over the road to the Windmill Ground pitch: a beautiful thing, fully enclosed, accessed through turnstiles, flood lit from all corners, perfect; a boy's dream to play in a theatre like this.

A generous crowd had gathered at the Windmill that evening. Eagerly anticipating some professional input, participating players not on the pitch sat in the dugout, being substituted in at regular intervals. It was great fun being so close to the action, and finally it was Lenny's turn for a run out. Although he didn't recognise any of the players as professionals, there was one ex-professional playing who everybody recognised – Jimmy Hill, Coventry City manager, and the owner of the sofa Lenny and Linda had eaten their chips on.

After that night, Lockheed became a hot topic for Lenny, and he enthusiastically recounted his experience to anyone who cared to listen. Dad's plan had worked – if Lenny was lucky enough to gain an interview, he knew his son would now give a good account of himself. But only time would tell whether that interview would be forthcoming.

# Interview

Back at Burgis and Colbourne, Lenny kept his mouth shut about the application. He continued to enjoy his work but not the twelve-mile daily trial. So he saved his cash, dreaming that one day he might be able to afford his own motorbike. Whenever he asked his dad if he'd be allowed to have one though, he was met with a stern no – and if Dad said no, it meant no. But this didn't stop Lenny dreaming, and the Kenilworth Chapter – now formed, but lacking motorbikes – arranged to hold an EGM to discuss a matter of great importance: it had come to the attention of one of the chapter that a motorbike licence could be applied for before your sixteenth birthday. Lenny, being the eldest, was chosen to be the guinea pig: he should get the forms and fill them out; the whole chapter were keen to see the result. Until then, they had to be satisfied meeting on foot or riding pushbikes.

Owners of motorbikes or not, the chapter met without fail on Friday nights as rockers. Lenny would sneak his leather jacket from the suitcase under the bed and slip it on, becoming what he longed for a couple hours. The lads would start the evening at Jim Tibbets's house, watching his dad tune motorbikes in the garage, then move on to the youth club for a couple of hours, before going for a chip batch at the Late Eat – the rockers' café of choice. The Late Eat's car park was ideal for motorbikes to roar in and out from, and the rockers there put on quite a show: Fingers Watkins on his Norton Dominator, Ron Holmes on a

Lightning and Mick Dolby with a C15. But it was Dale Crew's Thunderbird that took centre stand – a beautiful bike that everyone envied. Kenilworth's night air filled with stories about clashes in seaside towns – mods and rockers on their motorbikes and scooters – all firing Lenny's imagination in the hours before he had to pedal home and hide his leather jacket and his secret.

§

Several weeks went by and then a letter arrived in the post addressed to Lenny. It was an invitation from the Lockheed to come for an interview. Dad was most pleased; although in his heart, he thought Lenny stood little chance of success. He didn't want his son to be too disappointed, so he told Lenny that even the chief draftsman's son had been turned down for a place. The fact that Lenny was still only fifteen must have made him the youngest applicant, but Dad wanted him to give it his best shot and gain from the experience. So what should he wear for the interview? Dad thought black trousers would be fine, along with Lenny's old school tie, but that a trip to Burton's for a new sports jacket would help. Dad would have preferred a shorter hairstyle – Lenny had Beatle hair to match his Beatle boots – but it was the fashion and only to be expected.

§

When the big day arrived, the route Lenny had to cycle was a full two miles further than his current place of work. Having locked up his pushbike in the cycle shed, he reported to the police gate where he was directed along a boulevard towards the training centre. A receptionist welcomed the interviewees, who were then handed over to a secretary, who inspected their invitations, registered them and signed them in. All Lenny's other documents would not be required after all – including the school report – which came as some relief; the documents could be pigeonholed and collected later. The secretary explained that the Lockheed prided itself on its process of selection, reminding them that they only took the cream from the top.

When a group of five candidates had assembled, the secretary gave them an introduction to the company and explained the timetable for the day. They were to start with a tour, then take an examination, and conclude with an interview. So off they went. When it got to lunchtime, Lockheed provided the candidates with a free meal in the staff canteen, then it was back to the training centre to be examined. Over lunch, Lenny chatted to a fellow applicant called Dave, who had travelled all the way down from Liverpool on his motorbike for the interview. When Dave told Lenny he had taken his O-levels already, it took Lenny's breath away. What could he reply in return?

The first part of the afternoon examination was held in a classroom. Applicants were given an A4 booklet with their name on the front and told they had thirty minutes to answer as many questions as possible. Lenny didn't think the test was too bad, and it all made sense. Then they moved to another room for some practical tests, culminating with the Flash Light Challenge: each applicant was handed a box with a dismantled torch in it – they were to reassemble the torch to a working condition in a given time. The challenge being that the box also held parts that did not belong. After the allotted time had elapsed, Lenny's torch was shining bright, but not for all.

When the time for the interview arrived, Lenny was ushered in front of a panel of three: in the middle, peering over half-moon glasses, was head of the training centre, Mr Butterworth; to his left sat head of workshops; and to his right a personnel manager. The panel talked about the company, pointing out that Lockheed had facilities second to none and that they expected the very best. The interview seemed more of an examination of the paperwork laid out on the desk in front of them, with lots of page-turning and thumbing accompanied by a couple of basic questions.

Just as it seemed the interview was about to round off, Mr Butterworth said there was one last thing, and he posed a question as follows: on a standard one-bar electric fire, what does the green wire connect to? Lenny remained calm and thought for a moment, remembering a science lesson at school with Mad Ned, which had been about electrical circuits.

'The frame,' Lenny replied, 'providing an earth.'

The panel seemed happy with everything, and Lenny returned to reception, where he collected his folder and was told he would be contacted in a couple of weeks. Retracing his footsteps from earlier that day, he walked down the boulevard to the bike shed, where Dave was preparing to return home. Dave said if his application was successful, his Dad had promised to buy him a new motorbike and he'd be selling this one. Lenny said if they met again, he might just buy it. Cycling the eight miles back to Kenilworth, Lenny had plenty to think about, but the chance of getting a motorbike was topmost in his mind.

Back home, Dad wanted to know every detail of the interview, but it was like getting blood from a stone; now the day was over, Lenny's thoughts were on other things: Brian Warr, a successful local football coach, was forming a new U18 side to play out of

Kenilworth Working Men's Club. Brian was cherry-picking a team to challenge for honours, and he had come to speak to Lenny at the house to explain his plans for the new season, plans that had Lenny in a central role. Of course Lenny wanted to accept the offer, but there was a problem: as it stood he worked Saturdays, and in the week – by the time he had eaten his tea – it was nearly seven o'clock before he was free. Brian explained that training would take place either in the Abbey Fields or at Beehive Hill, kicking off first week in August and, if Lenny could make it, he would be most welcome.

# Game Changer

Towards the end of July, a recorded delivery arrived for Lenny. It arrived during the day, so it wasn't until six o'clock that he became aware of it. The large brown envelope sat in the middle of a cleared dining table, surrounded by his family, when he arrived home. All eyes were on the package, eagerly awaiting the contents to spill. The enclosed letter explained that Lenny had been offered a five-year indentured apprenticeship commencing on September 4th, his sixteenth birthday. All the necessary documents were enclosed and needed signing and witnessing and returning by hand or recorded delivery as soon as possible. Dad was beaming. He would handle it, he said, to make sure everything was done correctly.

This was an incredible achievement for a lad of fifteen without qualifications, a real game changer, but Lenny didn't realise it at the time. He felt settled in his job at Burgis and Colbourne and didn't really want to leave, but Dad reminded his son that he would be able to join Brian's new football team, and when he promised to take Lenny to Blackpool for a ride on the big dipper, this was enough to talk him into handing in his notice.

Given his new-found status, Lenny thought it might be worth having another go at Dad to see if he would let him have a motorbike. Lenny's chapter were all saying they would be getting bikes soon, and he didn't want to be left out. Lenny approached his dad, but Dad was having none of it; the media coverage of mods and rockers fighting had sparked moral panic about British youth, and Dad was on the side of those who described them as vermin and louts.

Another piece of hot post arrived at Lenny's house shortly after the envelope from the Lockheed: a provisional driving licence with a start date of Lenny's birthday a month away. This was interesting news for the Kenilworth Chapter and meant they could all apply for licences three months before their sixteenth birthdays during the coming year. Gordon, who worked at the motorbike shop, had gained permission from his Mum to purchase a motorbike that was on sale there, even though he was months away from gaining his licence. Owning a provisional motorbike licence meant that Lenny was eligible to ride any motorbike up to 250cc without a pillion. Gordon was purchasing a single-cylinder 200cc Triumph Tiger Cub. Gordon wouldn't be eligible to ride it for almost a year, but when the chapter got their heads together, they thought there was a way around that.

§

True to his word, Dad booked the last week of August off as holiday, with designs on Blackpool. He thought it would be a good idea for Lenny to hand in his notice to Burgis and Colbourne the week before, so the coast would be clear for his son to start at the Lockheed on September 4th. Until then, the days went by much as before. One lunchtime, however, prior to Lenny departing company with Burgis and Colbourne, Dad arrived at the store – something Dad had never done in all the time Lenny had worked there. He told Lenny he had some bad news: Jimmy Hill had resigned as manager of Coventry City Football Club. Lenny was shocked and couldn't understand why Jimmy would do this after taking them to the top – there are things that seem inexplicable to a young mind and leaving at the peak of your game is one of them.

§

With mixed feelings Lenny worked out his notice, and this gave him time to reflect before departing from Burgis and Colbourne. His time there had provided him with focus and stability, confidence and self-belief when most needed, and this must have played an important part in his selection by the Lockheed. For this Lenny would be forever grateful.

On his last day, Lenny supplied cream cakes to all the staff. He said his goodbyes and promised to visit. Then, with a handshake from Albert, the soon-to-be Lockheed apprentice departed the store, unable to look back for his eyes were filled with tears.

# Blackpool

Meanwhile back home, excitement was rising about the bank holiday treat with prospects riding high for a ride on the big dipper at Blackpool. The family were to travel north in Dad's Beetle, and when Lenny arrived home, Dad was checking it over whilst Mum finished packing.

Now according to Dad there were only two things you needed to know about Beetles: one was that they were totally dependable and would never let you down, the other that they provided only limited space for both passengers and luggage. This, however, did not delay the departure and soon they set off – Dad driving, Lenny map-reading, and Mum and little sister Julie crammed in the back with the luggage.

Having reached the Blackpool-side of Preston without a hitch, the Beetle suddenly died. After all Dad's preaching about dependability, all he was left with was 'limited space'. Seemingly stranded, with no prospect of help, Dad set to work to identify the problem... no spark! It turned out to be the condenser, a small thimble-sized electrical component. This was a difficult position for the family to be in and gave Dad little choice than to leave Lenny in charge and set off on foot to seek a solution. Dad couldn't remember seeing anything that might be of help on the road they had travelled, so gambled in a forward direction into the unknown.

After about three hundred yards, he came across a concealed gateway to an unmanned car pound, which he studied for a few minutes before returning to his Beetle. There he collected a couple of screwdrivers and his trench coat, which was always kept next to the spare in case of emergency – and this was one! Beckoning Lenny to follow, he returned to the pound – which was fenced off all the way round – threw his coat on to the barbed wire that ran along the top of the fence and clambered over into the pound where he had spotted a suitable donor.

The rear hood, which on an old VW Beetle covers the engine compartment, is secured by a push-button catch. Some models were not fitted with locks, and this was one, so all Dad had to do was press the button to open it and expose the engine. Within five minutes, he had removed the condenser and closed the hood again and, with Lenny acting as lookout, he clambered back over the fence and returned to the family car. Within minutes of their return, the condenser was transplanted from the donor vehicle and Dad's Beetle rose from the dead.

As it was the August bank holiday, Blackpool was pretty busy when they arrived. Most of the guesthouses displayed no vacancies signs, and it took a little time to find suitable accommodation, but eventually they got fixed up in a B&B a few roads back from the front.

Dad was keen to get a spare condenser, so he went sniffing round Blackpool for a garage. Mum, Julie and Lenny found the seafront and walked along the promenade. In the distance one way was the Blackpool Tower, in the other was the funfair. Seeing the big dipper made Lenny keen to get off on his own, and he didn't want Dad coming back and cramping his style, so it was down to the fair straightaway, telling Mum and Julie he'd see them later.

At the funfair end of the promenade, there were a lot of lads wearing leather jackets with motorbikes parked up alongside.

Lenny thought this was great and got chatting to a girl who was with them. She explained she was from the sky-blue part of Manchester and had come down with her brother and his mates for the day because they fancied a look around the fair. Lenny explained he was from the sky-blue part of Coventry and had fancied doing the same, so they paired off and went to have their fortunes told before enjoying a snog on the big dipper.

*Pic 4, Julie at Blackpool Tower Zoo.*

It was quite a way back from the funfair to the guesthouse, so when Lenny was offered a lift back up the promenade in a sidecar combo, he couldn't have been more pleased, and he also managed to avoid the guesthouse curfew.

Although Lenny didn't want to be seen with his parents because he thought they were the squarest things on the planet, the sentiment did not apply to his four-year-old sister Julie, who he had always loved and cared for. This bank holiday, they were sharing a room that was warm and unventilated and had brushed nylon sheets that made it difficult to sleep. After breakfast the next day, Lenny gave Mum and Dad some free time by way of taking Julie to the Tower Zoo where she had her photograph taken with a monkey. By lunchtime though, it was fish and chips on the seafront and home. The return journey went without a hitch, but there was *one* stop – when they reached the car pound that had saved the day, Dad pulled up in the gateway and popped an envelope in the postbox attached to the gate. When Lenny enquired what was inside, Dad replied, 'Two notes and a condenser.'

# Prohibition

With September 4th fast approaching, Lenny was looking forward to receiving a new pair of football boots for his birthday – although he had saved up some money, Dad had promised him a pair to start the new season with Kenilworth U18s, who had already started training at Beehive Hill. It should not come as a surprise, however, to hear that Lenny was *not* looking forward to the sixteen-mile-a-day tour to the Lockheed and back, and despite Dad's prohibition, the boy was still thinking of how he could procure a motorbike.

When the big day arrived and Lenny turned sixteen, Dad must have felt all his problems – rolled into one in his son – had been solved: the boy now had a future. Lenny, however, only felt it was a long pedal to work. He had worked out that during the course of his training he would cover over 27,000 miles. For now, he covered the first eight and locked up his bike in the Lockheed cycle shed.

The 1967 intake – more than sixty in number – gathered at the training centre, known as the Tud. It consisted mainly of lads from high school and grammar school who had completed their fifth year and gained qualifications, and there were a couple of students too. Lenny recognised one lad in the crowd. It was Dave from Liverpool, who said he was staying at the Lockheed hostel and returning home at weekends on his motorbike. Lenny was keen to know if he might still be selling his bike, and Dave told him he was; in a couple of weeks Lenny could have first refusal. As from that day Lenny was sixteen and could legally ride a motorbike on the roads, all he needed to do now was get one.

After the morning's introduction at the training centre, Lenny found himself assigned to a drawing office, which was to be his place of work for the first month. It had the atmosphere of a library and you could hear a pencil drop. Also he'd been given a list of requirements, including dos and don'ts. High on the list was enrolling for day release at Mid-Warwickshire Technical College but given his lack of qualifications, Lenny would have to catch up by attending night school too.

Twice a day – so regular you could set your watch by it – a woman would come into the drawing office pushing a trolley. Her bottom shelf carried biscuits and crisps while her top shelf transported a large aluminium flask containing hot tea. Within seconds of her arrival, everybody in the office had their mugs at the ready, and Lenny soon learnt to join their ranks.

Training whilst working staff-hours meant a finishing time of five o'clock for Lenny to begin his eight-mile pedal home to Kenilworth. After just one day, he could not imagine doing this for the next five years. There had to be another way, and hopefully it was just over the horizon.

# Beautiful Apparition

On the second Tuesday after he had started at Lockheed, Lenny had to enrol at tech. Fortunately, he had managed to get his night school to follow on straight after his day release. The tech was in Leamington, and Lenny preferred to travel there by bus, stopping at the top of the Parade and walking up. On his return, he would call in at the Tavistock chippie and have his tea while waiting for his bus home.

One autumnal evening, Lenny was enjoying the view from the upper deck while the bus passed the main entrance to the Abbey Fields in Kenilworth. As he gazed down, he spotted some old school friends with girls as company, from which one stood out, appearing to Lenny as a beautiful apparition – the most stunning girl he had ever seen. This was love at first sight. At the first opportunity, Lenny made enquiries about his apparition and found out her name was Maggie. Not knowing what to do by way of meeting her, he resigned himself to bide his time, instead spending his energies trying to make a case once more to Dad for buying a motorbike – citing the distance to and from work in his favour. But again it was no, followed by, 'If you get one, you will have to go.'

§

When the time came for Dave to sell his motorbike, he remained true to his word and gave Lenny first refusal. Lenny shook on the deal and Dave told him to come to the Lockheed hostel that Saturday morning to pick up the bike.

When Saturday came, Dave took Lenny to Jack Parker's insurance agent to get one-year cover – including fire and theft – for the cost of five pounds, then it was back to the hostel, where Lenny exchanged a further £20 for Dave's 200cc Norman single with logbook and keys. Finally Lenny was the proud and legal owner of a motorbike. With a grin on his face, he rode off towards Kenilworth, not worrying for the moment where he would garage his new mode of transport; like his jacket, he knew he would have to hide the bike. It was no good taking it home – Dad had made his point.

The answer came in the form of an old motel where Morecambe and Wise had once stayed, sited on the grounds of an Esso petrol station at the bottom of the Crackley Hill, near where Lenny lived. The motel had fallen into disrepair, and after making enquiries with the manager of the petrol station, Lenny arranged to house his motorbike there for free, as long as he bought his petrol from the garage.

Friday night was a must hang-out night at the youth club, where quite a crowd gathered. Being a learner motorbike rider meant you could not legally carry a passenger until either you or they had passed the test. But the big car park at the side of the youth club did not fall under this umbrella, and the Kenilworth Chapter assembled the next week to assess Lenny's motorbike along with his riding ability.

Eager to be part of the performance, they took it in turns to ride on the back. As a pillion passenger, you are required to sit up close behind the rider to keep the motorbike stable – should you sit away at the back of the saddle, it affects the balance and handling of the bike. Halfway through the night, Lenny's old classmate, Terry Shilton, was enjoying his stint at the back while unknowingly being accelerated across the path of an oncoming Hillman Imp, which was entering the car park. To avoid impact, both Lenny and the Imp swerved, but they both swerved the same way, resulting in a head-on crash and Terry being catapulted on to the bonnet of the car, nose pushed up against the windscreen, peering through the glass at the driver. Thankfully, to everybody's amazement, there was no real damage and all walked away unscathed.

Bike-ability was always a hot topic amongst the Kenilworth Chapter – being able to lay the bike over left or right while travelling at speed through bends was an exciting and much practised skill, along with wheelies and riding no hands. Soon, though, there was an even hotter topic to grab Lenny's attention: a new group of girls from the grammar school had started attending the youth club, and within it was Lenny's apparition. He was desperate to stand out from the crowd, desperate to get himself noticed, desperate to win her over. What should he do?

§

The Kenilworth Chapter thought it would be a good idea for Lenny to pass his motorbike test – as a learner he was restricted from taking passengers – so Lenny applied. The test centre was at the top of the Parade in Leamington Spa. Lenny didn't bother wearing a crash helmet to his test, in fact he didn't even own one, helmets not being compulsory in those days. The examiner gave instruction to ride round the block while making good use of hand signals. He said he would also expect Lenny to make an emergency stop when he raised his hand. All went well. After that there were a few Highway Code questions, followed by the word 'passed'.

The mechanics of a motorbike were becoming second nature to the Kenilworth Chapter, all meeting up down the Pepper Mines or round Jim's dad's garage by the youth club. Top speed and acceleration were always being debated, along with what could be done to improve a bike's performance. Top of this list was always to skim the head, which meant removing the cylinder head from the motorbike and getting it to an engineering workshop to machine off ten thousandths of an inch. When fitted back, it was thought this would raise the compression ratio of the engine; thus making it go faster – or at least that was the theory. In practice, it often knocked out the big ends and blew the engine. However, on this occasion, Lenny convinced himself it had worked, giving him an extra five miles per hour to take his top speed up to seventy.

Jim had now become the proud owner of a 200cc Ariel Arrow along with a set of L-plates. The bike had terrific acceleration, being a twin, and Jim was keen to demonstrate. He had just repaired a puncture, but while refitting the drive chain he had put the clip to the split link round the wrong way. When Jim opened the throttle and sped off down Bertie Road, the split link failed, instantly ceasing the engine and throwing Jim off into the youth club gardens. It was back to the drawing board for Jim.

§

Lenny's days of pedalling to work were over, but there was unrest at the Lockheed. Amongst the apprentices there was a pretty even split between mods and rockers, and things often got fractious, culminating in a red-hot mug of tea being thrown straight in one lad's face. Cyril Stokes, head of workshops, got the lads together and expressed, in the strongest possible terms, that should any outbreak of fighting occur, it would result in instant dismissal.

Tensions mounted, but good sense prevailed, and to resolve their differences, it was agreed instead to meet outside work to sort things out once and for all. Both parties met at 6am on Mill Passage – the footbridge spanning the river Leam – for the action to begin. On one side of the bridge were the mods, wearing their parkers, fronted by Pete Blakeman and Chris Taylor, on the other side were the rockers, in leathers, headed by Lenny and Johnny Mayer; both gangs carried their tools of choice ready to tackle any eventuality. The cold morning grew silent. The young men's breath misted the air, and the two sides eyed each other. Then they walked towards the centre of the bridge and cast off: the gang that caught the most fish in an hour were to be declared winners.

The result of this Great British Cast Off was that neither side caught any fish – both blaming the proximity of the weir and all claiming to have had big bites. An amicable draw was agreed and this seemed to amalgamate the lads, who from then on became quite good friends.

# Gatecrasher

Lenny had managed to conceal his motorbike from Dad, who still had no idea of his son's secret. Although questions were asked about the greasy oil on his hands, which was due to him constantly making adjustments to his machine, no one guessed; Lenny said the oil was down to the chain on his pushbike – claiming it kept coming off.

As for Lenny's apparition, Timmy got wind of a party round at Martin Leatham's house in Amherst Road. The word was it would be crammed full of easy-riders from the grammar school and convent. Timmy told Lenny to come round and pick him up but as they didn't have an invitation they would have to gate crash. Lenny was a bit early, so he decided to go for a spin down Inchbrook Road, which had a fabulous horseshoe bend and was great for laying a bike over. But Lenny misjudged it and came a cropper, dropping the bike down and knocking the heel clean off his Beatle boot. He picked up the bike and went to pick up Timmy. When he walked through Timmy's lounge, the family commented that he was walking with a limp, but he wasn't – he was just down one side for the lack of a heel.

Off they went to the party, but first Timmy fancied being taken for a spin up Crackley Lane. The night was turning out to be the foggiest, smoggiest imaginable and visibility was down to a few yards. Lenny thought the lane bent left, but it didn't – left was the entrance to a farm. They crashed into the farm-gate head-on, bursting it open and falling from the bike. Neither lad was hurt, so they dusted themselves down, got back on the bike and headed off to attempt a different type of gatecrashing. It turned out though, when they got to the party, they didn't need to crash at all: they were made welcome and asked in.

Entering the party, taking care not to be seen limping, Lenny immediately clapped eyes on his apparition: there was Maggie, the girl of his dreams! But to his horror, he soon found out she was going out with the party's host, a spoilt mod, who had just been bought a brand new 175cc Lambretta scooter for his birthday.

Despite this disappointment, Lenny decided to enjoy himself by way of chatting up a girl named Liz, who turned out to be Maggie's best friend. After the party, Lenny was keen to get back on the level, so first thing in the morning, it was down to the cobblers to get his Beatle boot reheeled.

§

Lenny was quite keen on Liz and hung around close to her house, often taking her off for a ride and ending up in Crackley Lane for a cuddle. Depending on a girl's attire, it was not always appropriate to sit astride but riding side-saddle took care of that and was the coolest of rides. Liz, with her perfect pins, wore a miniskirt along with a three-quarter-length beige coat, which being of light colour marked easily from greasy hands. Liz's dad suspected what was going on and he did not approve. One evening, he sprung a trap to catch the cuddling couple snogging up the lane. He ordered his daughter to get in the car, and as he drove off, Lenny could see he had one hand on the steering wheel and the other flaying her. This was the end of their short romance, but they remained friends.

Two things about being an apprentice were that you received training, but you only received a relatively low income. Running a motorbike, however, incurred costs and maintenance, so if any repairs could be made on a do-it-yourself basis, they would be done.

Lenny was having trouble with his front brake: it was squealing and not pulling up, and it soon became apparent that it needed relining. This meant removing the front brake shoes and having some new linings riveted on – problem being the bike could be laid up for a couple of days waiting for the linings to come. Lenny had a bright idea about how this could be overcome, and he put the wheel back in place without the front brake. Then after tea, he headed off for Timmy's house on Common Lane – which is a rather steep hill. Lenny applied the rear footbrake to slow down thinking it would do the job, but it had little effect, giving him no option than to decelerate through the gears while heading straight for the T-junction with Dalehouse Lane at the bottom. At the junction, the lad shot straight across the road and up a grass bank, through a hedge, and into a farmer's field, coming to a stop amongst a herd of cows – no bull – with the engine still running. It took quite a while to sort out the muddle, and there was more to come. Lenny's friend Timmy was a big lad, and this could affect a motorbike's performance. Later that evening, having extracted himself and the bike from the cow field, Lenny failed to account for his friend's weight and rode over a pothole with Timmy on the back, knocking out his back wheel, sending sparks flying and grinding the motorbike to a halt for a second time that night.

After a couple of days, Lenny's linings arrived and were fitted – and carefully tested, as he did not want a reoccurrence of the brake failure. Carrying that feel-good factor that accompanies a recent service or repair, Lenny now felt fired up to perform some wheelie skills in front of his pals.

At the front of the youth club in Bertie Road, there was a lawn with a flowerbed alongside the public footpath. It was on the road here that Lenny decided to demonstrate his latest bike abilities. With an audience in place at the entrance to the club, excitement was mounting as everyone knew they were in for a treat. Lenny sat astride ready for action with Jim riding pillion. Revving the bike to the max, determined to impress, Lenny dropped the clutch to do a fantastic wheelie, but when he pulled the bike up on to its back wheel, it slipped from beneath him and both lads were hurled off, leaving the bike to land in a rose bed, pivoting on its footrest and rotavating the garden. It took quite some time to bring this prickly situation back under control and the lads thought they had better work on that particular skill!

*Pic 5, Ant Stock on Abbey Hill alongside the War Memorial.*

It wasn't all wheelies and bikes – there was football too. Lockheed had some wonderful sports facilities, and it wasn't long before Lenny got training with the men and had a run out with the works' reserves. They played in a league that was very competitive against teams like Dunlop, Triumph and Jaguar, but Lenny's sights were firmly set on winning the Warwickshire Cup with Kenilworth U18s.

As they progressed through to the quarter-finals, special training measures were implemented for the young side. The team joined forces with Kenilworth Working Men's Club under the guidance of Bob Hope, a no-nonsense and relentless taskmaster. He soon had the team running up and down Abbey Hill and then, when they were tired, running up and down Abbey Hill again, each with a player on his back. The training session would not be over until the players had completed a session of weight training back at the clubhouse.

For a final test before the quarters, the young hopefuls were pitted against the full club side. The likes of Mick Ballard, who was being trialled by Coventry City, played for the club along with Dave Shilton, who knew every trick in the book and was a 'mayor' to play against. The lads could not have been better prepared for the matches to come.

Back at the youth club, the hot gossip was Maggie had split from her mod boyfriend, Martin, and was being consoled by a group of friends. Lenny had done all he could to try to get noticed, but he had no idea if it had worked. Maybe a change of tactics might help. A direct approach. But he needed to get Maggie away from her friends for a one-to-one. When at last she stood alone at the coffee bar, her mates having gone to the powder room, Lenny swooped, casually asking if she liked funfairs, then saying he might go to one up Campion Hills and did she fancy going? Lenny could see Maggie's friends were on their way back, and he felt the full flush of anticipation until her reply was yes. But in the excitement of the moment, Lenny wasn't sure if she had said yes to liking fairs or yes to going with him. Later he sought clarity through Liz, and it was yes to going. Bingo! The couple made plans to meet up at Elmdene Stores and go from there for their first date. Lenny rolled up on his motorbike wearing a leather jacket while Maggie got on wearing a three-quarter-length coat with sailor buttons, suitably attired to sit astride. Then it was off to the Hills. That first ride felt like being accompanied by an angel.

# Big Trouble

Lenny's motorbike was very popular with his mates, but there were only a few places where they might trial. One place they could have a go was on the dirt track at the Common, which also doubled as a pretty good hang out, being off the map of any authority. There was also Princes Drive, where Timmy's Dad had a warehouse; its service road was private, which meant it wasn't part of the public highway so traffic regulations didn't apply; the problem there were the neighbours whose houses backed on to the developing estate. Although the lads did not set out to deliberately upset anybody, it had become a regular occurrence.

One day the gang of three – Timmy, Lenny and Dick – were playing down the back with the motorbike. Dick had got hold of some new lead slugs, which turned out to be particularly deadly for pigeons, and the lads were taking pot shots with Lenny's air rifle. One unlucky bird tumbled down to land on a neighbour's veranda, and when the house owner retrieved it and brought it out as evidence, dropping it at the feet of the gang and informing them they were to be reported, the lads thought it might be a good time to hide the slugs and put the gun away. So then it was off up the railway to mess about some more.

With a plentiful supply of ammunition, what lad would not throw stones? First target was the water-filled pit, making a big splash, then the telegraph poles, and finally, the signal post, which rang out every time it was struck full on. Suddenly, the lads were surprised by the police, who came running up behind them. The cry went out to scarper and off they went pursued by the boys in blue. Dick and Lenny had fantastic running credentials, which made them uncatchable, and soon they were down the embankment and halfway across the field without breaking sweat. But when they turned to see Timmy's progress, the police had nearly caught up with him, arriving at the top of the embankment just as he was about to clamber over the fence at the bottom. Timmy looked for a place to climb, but before he could get a foothold, an officer took a tumble and rolled down the bank, colliding with his quarry and stopping their friend's escape. Dick and Lenny hid in the long grass watching and wondering how they could help, but all too soon, police back-up arrived and started hailing the lads with a megaphone.

'Come back! We've got your mate,' they cried. 'We know who you are!'

The lads knew the game was up and returned to face the music.

The officer who took the tumble was covered in green pigment and had been separated from his helmet, which was now residing in a bramble bush, and he was not a happy bunny.

In truth, the police didn't have much to go on but they were determined to make something stick, so all the lads' details were recorded and they were told a full report would be sent to the chief constable, but for now they would be reported for trespassing.

The lads didn't think it was that serious. Their antics had just been custom and practice. They had no idea what the police had in store, so when an envelope containing court papers arrived addressed to Lenny he kept them tucked away in his bedroom, not really understanding what they were all about. When the gang of three finally got their heads together, the reality of the situation began to dawn. They had been charged with trespass and criminal damage with intent to endanger life. Things looked pretty serious.

*Pic 6, Old Court House, Rugby Road.*

Timmy's parents were deeply shocked and had no intention of risking their son's liberty, so they transported him away to Austria to avoid the long arm of the law. No such luck for Dick and Lenny, though, who were due to stand trial within the month. Desperate for some friendly advice, Lenny returned to his roots and went back to Saint Nicholas Boys' Club to confide with Eric Teale the leader. Eric's instructions were to present himself in the best possible light: to be polite and to get dressed up smart for the occasion – definitely no leather jacket.

So Lenny turned up to court a smart rocker. He parked his motorbike round the back of the courthouse by the exercise yard, out of sight of the magistrates. Then he took the front entrance in from the Rugby Road to submit to due process. Dick was already inside with his dad, who immediately told Lenny things did not look good: a hard bench was sitting, and they were potting everybody. He told Lenny to report to the clerk of the court, whose job it was to make sure everything ran smoothly; clerks are fundamental to the justice system, advising magistrates, witnesses and defendants.

Reporting to the clerk, Lenny was asked whether he was the son of John Unsworth; the clerk had seen the surname and said he thought he knew Lenny's dad. Lenny confirmed he was and the clerk quickly moved on to enquiring whether Lenny was being represented. When the lad said he wasn't, the clerk judiciously suggested a duty solicitor might be a *very* good idea.

The duty solicitor explained that he needed time to study the case and the clerk indicated this would not be a problem; things need not be rushed and could still be concluded that day. The best results usually came after a tea break, he confided.

There was a lot of hanging about, then suddenly a burst of activity as the police, the solicitor and the clerk got together. Something had happened. The solicitor took Lenny to one side and explained the police would do a deal: they would drop the intent to endanger life charge if he and Dick entered a guilty plea. This was advisable, but the likelihood of a custodial sentence still loomed large. The lads thought they had little choice but to agree, and when the charges were read out – reduced to trespass and criminal damage – they both pleaded guilty.

The police outlined the facts of the case and Lenny's solicitor mitigated on the lads' behalf, telling the court they had no previous convictions and were of good character. The final word was given and the lads were offered the chance to speak. Dick declined, but Lenny accepted without hesitation. Standing in the dock, all eyes were trained on him. As the court fell to silence you could have heard a quill drop.

'I am deeply sorry for what happened,' Lenny said. 'I did not realise the damage or danger I caused by throwing stones and it will never happen again.'

Lenny returned to his seat and the court rose while the bench filed out to consider the sentence. When the bench returned, Dick and Lenny were told to stand as sentence was passed. Both lads were to be given one-year conditional discharge. This was an unexpected result and much better than anyone had hoped. Dick's dad said Lenny's public oration had saved the day, but he hoped they had both learnt their lesson. Lenny's dad, however, was yet to find out.

The press loved it, running headlines of "The Boy Who Said Sorry". Lenny's name appeared in the *Morning News* the following day, and by the end of the week it hit the *Kenilworth Weekly News*. However, due to press regulations, neither Dick nor Timmy's names were allowed to be printed as they were still under the age of sixteen.

Dad found out soon enough, but he remained silent – the signal to stay out of his way. Tension grew at home, and there was more to follow when an informant told Dad that Lenny had a motorbike, increasing the silence levels to a deafening, 'OUT!'

In some ways, it came as a relief that Lenny did not have to hide things anymore. He packed his little blue suitcase with his most treasured possessions and rode off to an uncertain future.

# Hospital Visits

Lenny's 200cc motorbike took him to Gordon's cottage in Ashow where his friend's mum had kindly offered him a bed – but only for a couple of weeks as she needed the room during the Royal Show. This gave Lenny a little breathing space and he thought he might be able to get fixed up with accommodation at the Lockheed works hostel, but he found on enquiry it was full. Even Maggie, who Lenny had only been seeing for a matter of weeks, said he could stay at her house, but he declined the offer thinking it might lead to complications.

The answer came when Dave Cook, a rocker from Arthur Street in Kenilworth, put up his 250cc Francis Barnett single for sale. Although it was only a 250, it had the look of a bigger bike, and that appealed to Lenny, so he agreed to buy it. During the course of their transaction, accommodation was mentioned and Dave told Lenny to have a word with his mum. Dave's mum said she would let Lenny stay for two pound ten shillings a week and that he could expect an evening meal in with the price.

It was the end of May, the time of year when people start to think about a bank holiday break and where it might take them. Gordon and Lenny were no exceptions despite the fact that one was fifteen and the other sixteen. Both had motorbikes and leather jackets, but Gordon was still too young to legally ride his bike on the road. They had heard that Yarmouth was a good place to go; mods and rockers ruled the seafront, and there was a big dipper too. Also, helpfully, Lenny knew the way as his Auntie Olive used to run a guesthouse in the nearby town of Gorleston. The lads decided to make the trip on Lenny's Francis Barnett, with Gordon sitting on the back carrying a large rucksack topped with their little green tent. It was one hundred and sixty five miles via the M1, past Newport Pagnell, and it rained most of the way, but even so it was fun getting there.

They pitched the little green tent on a soggy campsite field about two miles back from the seafront. The weather was not so good, but the lads thought it was great to be cruising up and down the seafront on the bike. At one end was the funfair, which had the big dipper, at the other, a pier; the two ends separated by the usual seaside attractions. The lads parked up and hung around the arcades and shops until they found themselves chatting to a couple of girls from Leicester, who they arranged to meet later.

Back along the front that evening, the couples met up and walked arm in arm to the fair, returning later, swept along by a romantic sea breeze, to the pier, where they sat amongst the shadows. Both couples exchanged details and the lads vowed to make contact on their return home and visit Leicester to meet. The next morning, when they met to say their goodbyes, the girls marked their departure with hugs and kisses, proudly wearing badges embossed with "I was a virgin".

The lads kept their word and visited Leicester a few weeks later, but the romantic breeze of Yarmouth's seafront was missing, and it turned out to be the last time the couples would see each other despite a couple of letters.

§

Lenny and Gordon's epic journey to Yarmouth was not without cost. It had taken a toll on the Francis Barnett, and its clutch was beginning to slip. Lenny's mate Dick had an instant solution – his uncle Pete had a 350cc four-stroke Triumph 3TA twin for sale on easy terms. Lenny thought this was great and a deal was done. No more two-strokes mix. Now he had a real machine.

*Pic 7, Triumph Bathtub*

The only problem with a 3TA was its nickname – the bathtub – because of its fully-enclosed rear end, which was no longer fashionable. So Lenny set about turning it into a sports: off came the old steel fairings to be replaced with shiny new alloy mudguards, but the most important thing to complete the makeover was a set of ace bars.

The 3TA had terrific acceleration and was capable of 80mph on a good road without suffering power drop when carrying a pillion passenger. But there was one exception.

Now the heat was off, Timmy had returned and had taken up employment as a trainee chef at the Abbey Hotel, which had a large car park to the side with a jitty separating it from Saint Nicholas C of E Primary School. During lunch break, Lenny would often nip back to Kenilworth and see Timmy. Saint Nicholas School had a picket fence, which all the kids – including Lenny's little sister Julie – would stick their arms through, waving at any passer-by. On the days Lenny came along Priory Road on his motorbike to see Timmy, it caused quite a stir. Pulling up, he would rev the engine and toot the horn, putting on a bit of a show for the cheering crowd. Unfortunately, the acting head was alarmed by its close proximity and initiated a showstopper, reporting Lenny to the police. The following day, a branch officer was stationed behind a tree on the opposite side of the road from the school. Lenny should have noticed his feet sticking out, but he was too busy looking for his little sister's attention. Having spent thirty minutes or so with Timmy in the Abbey Hotel car park, Lenny roared off, tooting goodbye and putting on a special demo for the kids. He snaked his bike from side to side while clapping his hands – a manoeuvre known as 'the wave', but this prompted the branch officer's immediate appearance. He stepped out centre stage to hail Lenny to a stop and brought the show to a dramatic end.

*Pic 8, War Memorial on Abbey Hill.*

This resulted in another appearance at the magistrate's court. Having recently been given a twelve-month conditional discharge for a criminal offence, Lenny had good reason to be worried. Fortunately, motoring offences did not invoke any previous orders so, for dangerous driving, Lenny received an endorsement on his licence and a five pound fine with time to pay. Again the press loved it and Lenny made the headlines of the *Kenilworth Weekly News* with "Look No Hands".

§

Cookie, Lenny's landlady's son, was a real showman. He had a 350cc BSA single fitted with monkey bars and wore an embossed leather jacket with a fringe. His was a very noisy machine that you could hear long before you saw it. Lenny preferred a racer look with ace bars and wore a plain leather jacket, ice blue jeans and Beatle boots, finished off with a white silk scarf. But they enjoyed each other's company, roaring round the streets of town, following in each other's wake.

Ninety-degree bends were of particular interest to the lads – seeing who could lay their bike over furthest to catch the centre stand and generate sparks was a ten pointer. Travelling up from the Kenilworth Clock to the war memorial, there is a ninety-degree bend with the additional hazard of adverse camber. One day, Lenny fancied spraying some sparks and laid his bike hard right, but his centre stand dug into some soft tarmac, spilling him across the road into the Abbey Fields, tearing his favourite ice blue jeans and grinding the skin off his knee cap, exposing the bone. Today there is fencing and a row of bollards by the war memorial entrance to the park, but in Lenny's day it was all clear, providing a grassy final landing for the injured boy. Even so, immediate medical attention was required, and this was given by a young woman who was passing. She had recently completed a first aid course and to Lenny's horror improvised a torque using his white silk scarf. Then it was straight over to Warwick Hospital for some professional care at A&E.

Lenny's knee developed an infection and required daily attention, but a big company like the Lockheed had their own medical centre and provided all the care he needed. Nevertheless, Lenny missed the attention he would have got at home from his mother and Julie, and lodging away started to seem a less attractive option. He was, after all, only sixteen.

§

Despite his knee injury, Lenny loved riding his Triumph. His preferred route to work was by way of Warwick Castle, crossing the River Leam, then along Banbury Road and up on Gallows Hill to Harbury Lane, a typical greenbelt back lane with grass verges and plenty of potholes.

One morning, a few weeks after his accident at the war memorial, Lenny was running a bit late. He got on to the straight section of the hill and throttled up to 70mph to overtake an old van, but when he cut back in he encountered a large pothole, which launched him and the bike into the air before dumping them on a wide grass verge. Tumbling, rolling, sliding, Lenny wondered if he was ever going to stop. Had he encountered a tree or telegraph pole, it would most certainly have been fatal. Lying in the long grass in a semi-conscious state, Lenny desperately needed hospital care yet again. The van driver was in a state of shock from what he'd just witnessed, but he had a difficult choice to make: should he leave Lenny lying there and go off to find help – there were no mobile phones in those days – or should he try to get Lenny in the back of his van to take him to the emergency department direct, which would more likely be quicker.

After a couple of minutes, Lenny became more coherent. As if coming round from a tranquillised state, he was able to make it into the back of the van with the driver's help. From there, the driver made A&E in quick time, pulling up at the front entrance and handing Lenny over to the nurses, who lifted him on to a trolley bed.

Inside the hospital, the lad was stripped down to his underpants and examined by a doctor, who seemed satisfied there were no broken bones or internal injuries. But Lenny's hands and face were shredded so, dressed in a white smock, Lenny was wheeled into theatre and placed on a slab under a large spotlight the size of a dustbin lid. At first, the warmth generated by the lamp was comforting and Lenny lay there dozing, but when the first needle went in, his eyes snapped open to see a huge, masked doctor stitching him up. Feeling in safe hands, Lenny closed his eyes for the duration, and after was left to slumber in a peaceful anteroom. Woken by a kiss on the cheek, the boy opened his eyes to see Dad, who said, 'Come home, Len. Come home.'

# Invincible

So Dad took Lenny home, discharged but fragile, to much fuss from Mum and Julie and, from there, Lenny sent message to Jim to see if he would help him recover his motorbike the next day. Jim said he would and together they went back to Harbury Lane to look the bike over. The only obvious problem, after removing all the grass and turf, was that the throttle cable had snapped at the handlebar end, leaving it dangling out of the carburettor. But the bike started okay and when Lenny pulled the cable up the engine revved. So Lenny rode the bike back to Kenilworth, pulling the throttle cable up between his legs. He dropped the bike off, then the following day went round to Cookie's to pack his little blue suitcase before returning to enjoy Sunday dinner back home with the whole family.

§

Lenny wasn't the only member of the Kenilworth Chapter to have difficulties at home or make a trip to the hospital at Warwick. Terry Shilton's dad had told his son to get out too, but – unlike Lenny – Terry had nowhere to go and he found himself sleeping rough in the play tunnels at Bates Memorial Park while the lads rallied round, visiting him with supplies of drinks and sandwiches. After a few nights of park life, Tes moved to the more comfortable accommodation of a hay barn close to Glasshouse Woods, but

Lenny still felt sorry for him so invited him back to his house for something to eat.

When Terry had finished his hot meal, he got on the back of Lenny's motorbike, ready to be returned to the barn, and off they roared, full throttle, up Crackley Hill. But when Lenny changed into third gear, there was a jolt and the power surged. Lenny thought there must be something wrong, so he glanced over his shoulder and saw Terry being dragged along the road behind the bike; his friend had slipped off the back and caught his foot between the footrest and exhaust pipe. Lenny immediately performed an emergency stop, leapt off the bike, and released Terry's foot, but when he turned to ask if his friend was okay, he found Terry's scalp had been ground off, right down to his skull. There wasn't a lot of blood, but there was a lot of raw meat and, like the van driver on Harbury Lane a few weeks earlier, Lenny was faced with a dilemma: should he stay or go for help? Without a van to load Terry into, Lenny decided to go for help. He raced home to fetch a dressing and ring the ambulance. Then he returned to aid his stricken friend lying at the roadside and wrapped his head in a large towel he'd grabbed off the line. Soon there were sirens and Terry was rushed to A&E.

When Terry was discharged from hospital, he was wearing the biggest head bandage the lads had ever seen. He resembled a mummy: his head completely wrapped up with just two holes to see through. Terry's dad immediately invited his bandaged son to give up barn life and return to the family home.

§

Despite the recent run of accidents, Lenny was still keen on his motorbike, loving the adrenalin rush of speed and the admiration of onlookers when he put on a show. He treasured the feeling of freedom it gave him – on his bike he could do what he liked and go where he liked; there was no Dad telling him what he could or couldn't do – and nothing was going to take that away from him. He felt invincible, and even when arriving at the Royal Oak, the site of a fatal bike accident, he would sweep past on the dangerous S-bend and wave at the crowd outside before returning to park up.

One evening in the early summer, Lenny was inside the Oak enjoying its cheap, rough cider at one and three a pint, when an old class mate, James Douglas, pulled up outside. At school, the lads used to sit together in the art room, drawing pictures of motorbikes and dreaming about doing the ton. When Lenny came out of the Oak, he was surprised to see James sat astride a Triumph 3TA, which coincidentally was the same model as Lenny's. The two decided to put their bikes to the test to see who was best.

They set off with a roar to tour the outskirts of town, taking it in turns to follow in each other's wake, the bikes sticking like glue to the tarmac on that warm summer evening. They rode through Crackley bends up to Gibbet Hill for the speed trial down the straight mile, and there they raced, side by side, along the wide straight Kenilworth Road. It was neck and neck all the way and remained so at the finish, the result not being disputed. Their dream of doing the ton, however, remained elusive.

Another school friend that Lenny hadn't seen for a while was David Bowdler, who was about to join the army to study music and become a bandsman. When the two friends bumped into each other unplanned, they decided to have a night out together to rekindle their friendship. Dave asked Lenny to meet him by the prefabs rather than at his house, as his dad, like many of the others, didn't approve of motorbikes.

When Lenny picked him up, Dave was wearing a black leather jacket and had made an attempt to seem older by pencilling in his moustache and sideboards. The idea was to find a pub that would serve sixteen-year-old lads beer. Lenny thought he would give Dave the thrill of the straight mile so he let rip along the Kenilworth Road, then throttled back to cruise around Coventry close to the football ground. Here there were lots of backstreet pubs and the lads crawled along until they found one suitable. They parked up outside and went in to enjoy a pint of mild while chatting about their past and future. On departure, while preparing to mount, the lads were approached by two ladies of the night who enquired if they wanted a bit of business. The lads politely declined the invitation and rode off, feeling lucky to have got away without it. Flat out back up the straight mile, Lenny carried Dave to his drop-off point by the prefabs with Dave's dad none the wiser.

# Top of the World

With the prospect of the U18 Warwickshire Cup Final just one match away, Kenilworth U18s pulled out all the stops in preparation for their semi-final. It was not clear who would be in the team or where they would play until the last minute, but when the team list was finally pinned up on the noticeboard, Lenny was pleased to see his name in the middle of the sheet in the position he had been training for.

The semi-final was not a pretty affair, but Kenilworth's strength and fitness won the day to see them through to the final where they would be pitted against the current cup-holders from Coventry. To have got this far in their first season together was a fantastic achievement, but could they go one step further?

Kenilworth U18 football team were not just playing for a cup. There was the pride of their hometown at stake and it had been mentioned by Brian Warr that there could be scouts at the match and not the dib, dib, dib variety – these scouts had connections with some of the big professional football clubs and could recommend players they had seen for trial. Whether this was true or not was unknown, but it all sounded very exciting and gave the lads more to play for.

The clubhouse was not always available for the team's convenience, so a meeting room was arranged at Howard Ballard's house in Hyde Road. There the team's formation and tactics were finalised, with tips given by Howard's older brother Mick, who was being trialled for Coventry City. Mrs Ballard provided pots of tea for the lads to enjoy and there were plenty of biscuits.

The match was the talk of the town. The local press described it as the biggest game ever to be played by the town's young men, and the council gave special permission for the dressing rooms to be opened up at the swimming baths so the teams could change. The town's huge premier pitch alongside the war memorial was the venue for the day's cup final, with two coach loads of away supporters disembarking alongside in Forrest Road.

The current cup-holders were a tough City side, loud and confident, and they fully expected to retain their trophy – they had brought champagne on ice with them ready to pop at the after-match celebrations. In contrast, the Kenilworth team did not say a lot in the changing rooms. They felt a little overwhelmed by the occasion. Nevertheless, they were quietly confident and couldn't wait to kick off. The team had been announced back at the clubhouse and everybody knew what was expected of them. Brian gave Lenny last minute instructions – he was to play middle of the park. His orders were to win the ball and knock it wide for Ron Haydon playing left wing and Paul Nicholls on the right – these were to be Lenny's targets.

That huge football field alongside the war memorial had quite a slope and Kenilworth found themselves kicking against it during the first half with Brian screaming at Lenny for playing too deep. But it was difficult to get forward because of the pressure being applied by the opposition. On one occasion when they did manage to penetrate, Lenny put Paul through only to see him blast the ball over the bar, resulting in some factory language from Brian.

By half-time, Kenilworth were a goal down and had a couple of players struggling having taken knocks – in those days substitutes were not allowed; an injured player was expected to soldier on. During the break, the trestles were erected in preparation for the after-match ceremony, and the trophy now stood pride of place. The lads couldn't help but notice and this was a bit of a distraction. Brian got annoyed because he thought that some of the team were not listening to his instructions during the half-time team talk, so he abandoned the technical stuff and pointed at the cup. 'That's what you're playing for,' he told them. 'Now go out and f-king win it.'

*Pic 9, U-18 Gold Medal.*

Kicking down the slope in the second half, Lenny felt he was taking control of the midfield, finding Paul and Ron outside and creating chances and soon the goal came to draw level. Kenilworth had the momentum, and, in front of their home crowd, pushed forward until the opposition crumbled, leaving the Kenilworth boys to lift eleven gold medals and a silver cup and be crowned U18 Warwickshire Champions. Lenny was the youngest Kenilworth lad in the side that day, and for this English team, following in the footsteps of their heroes in 1966, it felt like they were champions of the world. Well they were!

Being good at something is not always a blessing. As much as Lenny liked his work, he would have happily given it up the next day for the chance of playing professional football. As far as Dad was concerned though, it would have been a terrible mistake to give up an apprenticeship in pursuit of an improbable dream, but when Manchester City came knocking, it was dream on. Brian had arranged for Lenny to be trialled at Manchester and he was told to take his boots and head north.

The boy could not have been more excited as he got changed in the home dressing room at Maine Road. He'd been on for about ten minutes and had not done much when he got on to a loose ball and scrambled a goal, but in doing so he collided with the upright, cracking his wrist. That was game over for Lenny, but he was first back into the dressing room to enjoy a swimming-pool-sized hot bath all to himself. He hoped scoring a goal might have got him noticed, but he would have to wait and see.

# Brighton Rock

A typical British motorbike leaked oil like the Torrey Canyon and Lenny's was no exception. His Triumph 3TA had a separate oil tank to feed the big end bearings with a cap that could be removed for filling or inspection. Dad had started to take some interest in the bike, and when he checked the oil one day in August, he noticed white flecks of metal floating in it. This could only mean one thing: the engine was on its way out.

*Pic 10, BSA 500cc Shooting Star.*

Lenny knew a guy named Les Rose who worked at Lockheed in the test department, and who just happened to have a 500cc BSA Shooting Star for sale. When he heard Lenny was looking for a bike, he invited him round to his house in Kenilworth to take the BSA for a test ride. Lenny liked the bike with its chrome petrol tank, but thought the asking price of forty pounds was a bit steep. Then he remembered Dad said never to give the full asking price, so he offered thirty five, which was agreeable and he left the owner of a Shooting Star.

Lenny now boasted the biggest bike in the Kenilworth Chapter, but not for long. No sooner had he worked out the gears than Jim turned up on a 500cc Velocette in mint condition. And that was not all – at long last Gordon was legal and could ride on his own licence. The surprise package, though, was John Tallis with his 250cc Yamaha. This machine could do anything plus more than most British 500cc bikes could do and it didn't leak oil!

So it was time to see how they would do in a speed trial down the straight mile. It was dangerous to ride three abreast, so four was pushing it, especially if you landed the inside lane, which had the added hazard of potholes, and after Lenny's close acquaintance with one of those, he now preferred the crown of the road. Sunday morning was the best time to trail as the roads were quiet with everybody in church, and so it was arranged.

*Pic 11, Straight mile.*

Travelling in a Coventry direction from Kenilworth, there were two things to know about the straight mile: one, that it was straight; the other, that it started with a descent down from Gibbet Hill that seemed to thrust a bike forward, giving added propulsion while accelerating away. After that, it was down to the bike to see how fast it would go and down to the rider to see how fast he dared.

The next Sunday, the lads tore along the empty road, four abreast, none of them holding back, each pushing their bike to its limit, but none of them reached the ton. After the trial, it was back over Gibbet Hill – which in days gone by had not been a good place to hang out – and down to the car park at the Coventry Cross pub for a debrief.

Taking into account dodgy speedometers, bouncy needles and wild exaggeration, the general consensus of the Kenilworth Chapter was 90mph, which was pretty hair-raising but not the ton they desired. Even so, the gang were very pleased with their new bikes and Jim suggested, with wheels like these, the ultimate test of man and machine must surely be a trip to Brighton. Lenny was more than up for it so plans were laid for the two lads to head to the south coast on the next holiday break.

Top of the list of equipment was the little green tent, followed by a WWII rucksack stuffed with the essentials of a primus, spam and beans. Also, Lenny felt it was a wise move to have a good selection of box spanners in case roadside repairs were needed and, of course, a map.

Brighton had gained notoriety during the Sixties when hundreds of mods and rockers clashed along the seafront. The lads were not expecting any of that, just the challenge of the ride there and back and a little recreation. Nevertheless, it all sounded very exciting and the boys couldn't wait to get down to the coast to see for themselves. Self-reliance was the order of the day – there were no ATMs or mobile phones, just a bit of cash in the pocket and a warm summer adventure ahead of them. The idea was to drop down to Southampton then take the coast road to Brighton, a trip of around two hundred miles. This was going to be some burn up!

When the day for the trip arrived, they took it in turns to lead so the slipstream advantage alternated equally between them as they settled to cruise south at around 70mph. Jim's all-black Velocette and Lenny's black and chrome Shooting Star must have made quite a picture cruising through the English countryside on this glorious day. Mid-point refreshments found the lads in a pub car park enjoying a cheese and onion batch washed down with a pint of rough cider. Their cruising technique was by now finely honed to take them across the rolling chalky downs to within touching distance of the coast. Then, on sight of the sea, they turned east in the direction of their destination and throttled down to suit the busier traffic conditions and soak up the beautiful scenery. This felt just great.

But when the lads started to get close to Brighton they noticed signs saying "No Motorbikes or Scooters". And when they got into town, there wasn't exactly a band playing to welcome them either. First port of call was the chip shop, where the owner was friendly enough, but then it was off again to find somewhere to camp. They hadn't spotted anywhere suitable on the way into Brighton, so the only choice was to look for somewhere on the way out.

Mile after mile of disappointment followed all along the coast. Then, after about thirty minutes, they came upon a small coastal town called Seaford. Things here seemed a little more laid-back and welcoming than Brighton, but there was still no sign of anywhere suitable to camp. With their motorbikes parked up, the lads had a walk along the front, drawing the attention of a group of teenage girls, who followed them round while dancing to pop music from their portables. The lads assumed the girls to be holidaymakers but, when they got chatting together, they found they were locals. Jim and Lenny were starting to feel a bit desperate given the fact that they had not yet found anywhere to pitch the little green tent, but the girls thought they may have a solution.

Escorting the lads away from the front towards a green about the size of a football pitch – with toilets as a convenience and the luxury of a chippie nearby – the girls said it would be okay to camp there, but the lads very much doubted it. The girls were so adamant that the lads thought they had no other choice, so they pitched the little green tent, generating quite a bit of local attention while a football match developed with all the kids. When the local bobby rolled up on his bike, they thought the game was up, but it turned out he was friendly and he took to the lads, sympathising at the lack of campsites. He told them their tent would be okay on the green for one night and he would keep an eye out for them.

So Jim and Lenny went back into Brighton, which was about a thirty-minute ride, parked up and had a pint, but the place was crawling with police and this made them uncomfortable, like they were being watched, so after a while they returned to the friendly little town of Seaford, where the girls were waiting to make them more than welcome.

The lads felt pretty pleased with what they had achieved, but realised they had come a long way, so they decided the next morning they would break camp and make a steady return home.

It was a perfect motorbike-riding day, but there was a lot of slow-moving traffic along the coast road, which caused the motorbikes to run a bit hot. The lads had been looking forward to the rolling hills and clear roads north of Winchester, where they could finally open up, but instead there was a bang followed by a cacophony and Lenny's engine died to silence. This event could accurately be described as a catastrophic engine failure, in the middle of nowhere, one hundred miles or more from home.

The motorbike had not stopped in the best place, but there was a layby up ahead, so Lenny pushed it there and put the bike on the centre stand ready for examination. Then they set about like never before to make a logical evaluation of the situation. Taking all things into account, they thought the best thing to do was to find out exactly what had broken inside the Shooting Star, so they set up a roadside workshop, laying out their tools with surgical precision and began an internal inspection by removing the spark plugs and inserting a screwdriver while turning the engine over with the kick-starter. The result showed that the right-hand piston was not moving up or down; the conclusion being that the connecting rod was broken or the piston had come off. To actually get inside the engine was going to take a little more than removing spark plugs: the cylinder head would have to come off, and this meant first removing the petrol tank, followed by extraction of the cylinder head bolts; after that, the head would have to be removed to expose the piston tops.

All this they did, and finally they could see the problem – when the engine got cranked over, the pistons should have gone both up and down, but the right-hand piston appeared to remain stationary at the top of its stroke. Prising at it with two little screwdrivers, Lenny popped the piston top out, which had clearly broken off from the main body and was now free to travel up and down.

After a few minutes assessing their findings, the lads thought there to be no good reason why a twin-cylinder motorbike should not run on a single cylinder, so they gave it a go. They set about reassembling the engine – minus the broken piston top – and isolating the right-hand cylinder from the carburettor by leaving out the pushrods. However hard they tried though, it seemed impossible to get the cylinder head back on and laying flat. Time for a cup of tea.

Out came the primus and, while waiting for the kettle to boil, they tried one last time. Suddenly, for no reason they could see, everything laid flat and the cylinder head could be bolted back down nice and tight. With the petrol tank back on, it was time to test. Apprehensively, Lenny tried kicking it over, then Jim had a go, but nothing much happened, so they tried altering the carburettor settings. There was a strong smell of petrol, which seemed to indicate the engine had flooded. To remove a spark plug and remedy this is quite a simple operation, but while it was out, Lenny decided to dry off the plug over the primus. He had got this tip from watching Dad when he had trouble starting. And it worked! The bike spluttered to life and Lenny was able to take it for a test ride. The bike was good going downhill but could barely make it back up to the brow; however, a few more adjustments seemed to improve the power enough to make a run for home. The lads thought that weight might be an issue, so Jim took the luggage and tied it to the back of his bike with the plan to take it one mile at a time.

On the flat, the Shooting Star managed 20mph, downhill, about 40mph, but uphill the speed reduced to walking pace and sometimes Lenny even had to get off and push. Jim started to fear that his bike might overheat, too, so he would let Lenny go ahead for twenty minutes, then catch up with him to see how things were going. They kept this shuttle going for the next six hours: Lenny's Shooting Star slogging mile after mile after mile and finally limping into town to two massive sighs of relief.

Within one week the Shooting Star was twinkling again, rebored and fitted with oversized pistons, express services supplied by Gordon Fortnum, and parts by his employer, Jack Parker Motorcycles of Leamington Spa. Lenny was back on the road.

# Good News

Further education for apprentices usually meant day release to a technical college while working the other four days. However, things were different at the Lockheed who had their own training centre with facilities better than most technical colleges. Lockheed apprentices were required to spend their first year in the training centre, so day release for them meant five days of training where apprentices at other firms received only one. Night class options were also available and Lenny had been attending these since the previous September. Exams had been sat and results were eagerly anticipated. When the results finally dropped through his door, Lenny was pleased to find he had passed and, not only that, he had passed with credits.

*Pic 12, Lenny.*

Towards the end of that first year at the Lockheed, there was to be an annual prize-giving event held in the sports and social club ballroom. This presentation was to showcase the year's achievements while demonstrating Lockheed as a top company to attract the best students from all over the country who were considering a career in engineering. The guest list consisted of principals from schools and colleges, union top brass, captains of industry, and special guest, Knight and Industrial Relations Specialist and Conciliator, Sir Jack Scamp.

When the evening arrived, the VIPs sat on stage behind neatly-arranged tables, facing a microphone and the audience. The apprentices had been told to dress smartly and wear a tie – all were expected to attend and, along with the public and press, it made quite a crowd.

Sitting at the back of the room with Dave and a couple of mates, Lenny expected no involvement whatsoever in the presentation; he felt relaxed and happy, just planning to have a good time. Then suddenly, he recognised a face on the platform. For a few moments his eyes were transfixed on this figure – it was none other than Lenny's nemesis, Dorothy Parncut, Principal of Kenilworth School. As the shock subsided, he realised she could do him no harm, to her he was just another face in the crowd. So he let out a breath and set about to enjoy the evening's proceedings.

First, the master of ceremonies, making full use of his microphone, introduced himself and the guests. Then, he moved on to categorise each and every award, inviting recipients up on to the stage to receive their prize from a VIP. The prize-giving was followed by speech-delivering – from several guests – and finally, in conclusion, the main event of the evening, a talk from the Conciliator himself, Sir Jack Scamp.

His theme was "The Next Generation of Engineers" and he concluded his inspiring speech with an announcement that there would be one final award – Young Apprentice of the Year. The hall became hushed and everyone looked round at the apprentices, wondering who would win. Sir Jack delayed the moment, ramping up the suspense, and Lenny considered which of his fellow workmates would claim the prize, not daring to think that *he* could be that apprentice walking on stage in front of the entire workforce and his ex-headmistress.

But then Dave nudged his arm.

'Leonard Unsworth,' Sir Jack called again.

And Lenny, not quite believing it, was ushered up to the stage and presented to the knight himself. This was a bolt from the blue, and not just for Lenny, who felt particularly pleased that a certain Kenilworth School guest was present. Sir Jack Scamp and the Young Apprentice of the Year shook hands and posed for the press, and when the photo appeared on the front page of the *Morning News*, Lenny was pleased to be featured in an issue he could proudly show his dad.

§

Sports and social clubs were very popular at big works during the 1960s and there was barely one mile separating Lockheed from a company called Flavels, whose club boasted a Friday night disco. Gordon and Lenny heard it might be worth a visit, so the next Friday, the lads burned up on their motorbikes to the dimly lit car park at the rear of Flavels' club.

Social clubs were usually a pretty safe environment, self-policed by committee members, but unbeknown to the lads, their leather jackets and motorbikes had drawn the attention of some local mods who had gathered outside. Having been in the club for an enjoyable hour or so, the lads were approached by two girls who suggested it might be a good idea to go outside and have a break from the loud music. Thinking they had pulled, the lads followed them down the steps and into the car park. But it was a honey trap. The girls melted away to be replaced by the mods.

What followed next was unprovoked. Gordon received a bloodied nose and a good kicking, while Lenny managed to keep his feet and ward off the attack. The mods finished by knocking the motorbikes to the ground. There was no damage to the bikes, and compared to the injuries the chapter frequently sustained in riding accidents, the bruises soon faded and all that was left injured was their pride.

# Superbike

Having successfully completed his first year training, it was time for Lenny to move into the working environment of the Lockheed. By being placed in various sections of the company while attending day release, experience was gained.

Lenny was placed in a department called Centreless Grinding. The foreman, a man named Eric, was in the process of purchasing a three-wheeled Reliant, which required only a motorbike licence to drive. Currently, Eric's mode of transport was a 700cc Royal Enfield Constellation – described as the first superbike – which had a sidecar attached to it. Lenny was quick to show an interest and, as Eric just wanted rid, he said the boy could have it for forty pounds. Lenny reasoned he could fit the sidecar to his Shooting Star and sell it on, leaving him with a superbike that may just do the ton.

Riding a combination was very different from riding a motorbike. It required experience that Lenny was clearly lacking. Having sealed the deal with Eric in the works' car park, a careful ride home through the back lanes seemed to make sense to the lad. He wasn't fully legal in terms of insurance, but he took the risk to get the bike and sidecar home. He had made it to Rocky Lane without incident, but when he let out the clutch, thinking the tricky part of the ride over, the sidecar flipped, turning the bike on its side. Lenny just managed to yank his leg out before it was crushed, but undeterred he set the combination back on its wheels and rode the last few miles home without further incident.

Straight after tea, Lenny was out into the garage to separate the combination – by now, Dad had consented to allow him full use of the garage as the Beetle was parked on the drive. It was hard work, but Lenny had become an expert mechanic, and when he was finished and stood back to survey his work, there on its centre stand stood the boy's very own British superbike.

The following morning, a more-than-pleased Lenny visited Jack Parker's to get insurance cover, and within an hour was out on the road astride his new bike. With its huge chrome petrol tank, the Royal Enfield looked a brute of a machine and had a roar to match – something Lenny liked very much to demonstrate – and when it came to acceleration the bike could take on anything and win, but there was a reason for that, which Lenny was not yet aware of. But what about the top end? Would it give Lenny his ton?

He took the Constellation to the Kenilworth Road.

And the straight mile gave its answer.

A disappointing 95mph.

This was a superbike. Was there a fault with the speedometer? Or was it something else?

§

For the time being, Lenny forgot about the top end and concentrated on getting his Shooting Star married to the sidecar to get back some cash. This was not a straightforward operation as the Star had not really been designed to be a combination, but eventually everything fitted together and was ready for a test.

Lenny's little sister Julie and her friends volunteered to be the dummies, and they all excitedly piled into the sidecar to enjoy rides around the block, which Lenny gave them without incident.

There was no rush to sell the Star – Lenny had an insurance policy that qualified him to ride any bike he owned – and now it had the bonus of being able to carry five – though not comfortably – but this was a price his passengers were willing to pay for a good night out. Top of the list was Brandon Speedway to support the local team called the Bees. Its car park spilled over with motorbikes, with many chapters converging, Kenilworth included, and it was quite a spectacle. Another outing during those weeks was the fair at Coventry's Memorial Park, not for the dodgems or waltzers, but to see the Wall of Death.

It wasn't just Lenny who owned a combination. Alan Shown, who had become a three-wheel fan after an accident on two, had the latest Japan had to offer: a 400cc Honda with a sleek, futuristic-looking sidecar. Both lads were keen Coventry City fans and Alan popped round one evening to invite Lenny to an away fixture due to be played at Stoke City that night. Lenny, however, had only just been served his cooked meal. Alan told him there was no time to eat – they wouldn't delay the kick off for that – so Lenny put on his jacket while getting into the sidecar and Mum handed him a tray laid with his meal to enjoy on the way.

During this time, three wheels became popular, and not just on motorbike combinations. Three-wheeled vehicles had a couple of distinct advantages over cars: one being that the driver did not have to pass a driving test, the other, that the road tax was cheaper and the vehicles very economical to run. This all appealed to Lenny's cousin, Frank Heston, who obtained himself a

Messerschmitt – a three-wheeled car made in Germany at the factory where ME 109 fighter planes were built during the Second World War. Legend had it the Messerschmitt's were built from surplus cockpits from the 109s, but whatever they were built from, it produced a quirky 200cc three-wheeled vehicle that boasted 57mph and 87mpg. Unlike the Reliant, the Messerschmitt had two wheels at the front, and some models even had tandem seating – with the passenger sitting behind the driver like in the cockpit of a plane. But the Kenilworth Chapter's romance with three wheels was over almost as soon as the word was out that Lenny's combination was up for sale. The Star with its sidecar was snapped up by three greasers, who arrived to test-ride it and then happily paid the asking price of fifty pounds.

*Pic 13, Messerschmitt.*

With some money in his pocket, Lenny set out to fix up the Constellation to his requirements. A set of drop handlebars were a must, closely followed by a new front tyre as the current one was square-edged and no good for handling. Once that was done, it really did feel like a superbike, so it was back to the straight mile. But the ton remained elusive.

Despite its failure to reach 100mph, the acceleration on Lenny's superbike was breathtaking, and this was demonstrated one evening after a chip batch at the Tahiti rockers café in Leamington Spa with Jim riding pillion because his bike was in for repairs. Leaving the streetlights of Leamington to return home along the Kenilworth Road, the lads were soon caught in the full beam of a car speeding up behind them.

'Great!' Jim shouted in Lenny's ear. 'A race!' And Lenny, needing no encouragement, pulled back the throttle and raced the bike over the notorious Blackdown Crossroads, easily opening up the distance between them and the glaring headlights. After Chesford Hill, Lenny throttled back – he had proved his point – and allowed his opponent to catch up, glancing at it as it arrived at speed and passed him on the right. It was a Jag. And not just any Jag. A Jag with POLICE blazoned on the side.

Quick to avoid any suggestion of racing, the rockers listened with humble accord. However, it soon became evident the police were going to bring charges. They said Lenny was speeding: doing 40mph in a 30mph limit. Then, after a thorough examination of the bike, they added the charge of 'no horn'. All this came as some relief – the charges didn't sound that bad. Not until the dust had settled did the full implications become apparent. Both charges carried endorsements and, when added together on Lenny's current licence, would take him to four, which meant a three-month riding ban. This prospect horrified Lenny and he sought professional advice from David Charlton, a local solicitor.

In the solicitor's opinion, endorsements were mandatory and unavoidable, but the court had discretionary powers to allow an offender to keep his licence if there was a case for hardship. Lenny thought professional representation to be too costly and that it would not be worth it in a case like this. He decided, from past experience, that the best course of action would be to represent himself and speak from the heart.

§

Since his last appearance at the magistrates, Leamington had built a brand new courthouse with all the latest security features. Offenders who had been summoned to court had to report to the clerk, who would call them when their case was due to be heard.

Having been called, Lenny listened to the police read out his case. It did not sound too bad. When he was asked how he wanted to plead, the boy answered that he was guilty. The magistrate nodded and asked if there was anything he wanted to say before sentence was passed. Lenny replied he was sorry for what had happened. He had not realised his speed, he said, and he didn't know he had to have a horn on. This caused a ripple in the press box, but they were told to keep quiet.

For the two offences, Lenny received a ten pound fine and two endorsements. There would also be a three-month driving ban unless there was any good reason the court might consider otherwise. Given this opportunity to speak, Lenny was sworn into the witness box where he explained to the bench that, as far as work and education were concerned, a driving ban would be very disruptive as he did not live on any direct bus routes. The bench retired for a second time and on their return ordered Lenny not to be banned, due to hardship. Mounting his bike outside the courthouse, Lenny felt very lucky to be riding away with a valid licence in his pocket, but the next day, when the newspapers carried the headline "No Horn On", Lenny wondered if he would be packing his bags again. He prepared himself to confess, but his dad never brought the matter up and the little blue suitcase stayed under his bed.

Lenny had experienced a run of lucky escapes – both from the law and from serious injury. He had a superbike and a beautiful girlfriend; even his Dad was coming on side. And for the moment he felt untouchable.

# King of the Road

The following spring, the hot chapter news was that Gordon had got himself a 650cc Pre-Unit Construction Triumph Bonneville and was claiming to be king of the road. This increased the urgency for Lenny to find out why his Constellation was under-performing at the top end and over-performing at the bottom. The answer, he discovered, was gear ratio. The Constellation had been geared up to run with a sidecar, not as a top-end racer, and the remedy would require a standard rear-wheel sprocket. The part took about a week to arrive and when it turned up was quite tricky to fit – Lenny had to remove several links of chain and take care to put the split link back in the correct position. Although the Constellation appeared to have lost a bit on acceleration, this was barely noticeable and now the bike was ready for a top-end test. Only ever having been close to the ton, there was no denying a degree of apprehension as to what lay the other side.

There was usually a lull in the traffic, after tea, during the six o'clock news, opening the way for a possible speed trial. To avoid any disturbance that evening and remain focused, Lenny pushed his motorbike away from the house to kick-start the engine at the end of the drive before warming it up with a spin around town. Everything seemed to be running smooth and sweet, so an approach to Gibbet Hill at the Kenilworth end of the straight mile was on. Turning the forks damper down fully to aid a fast ride, things looked set, and with favourable conditions being met at the brow of the hill, Lenny made a snap decision to open up and see what this superbike could really do.

Taking full advantage of the gradient, Lenny launched off along the straight mile. Screwing back hard, for peak revs in top gear propelled the Constellation into the nineties, pulling ever closer towards the ton. And then past it. 105mph! And there was more to give! But the road was running out and Lenny had to use every trick he had learnt to control this thundering beast of a bike. Throttling back through the gears, he slowed the Enfield down. He had done it. He had achieved his dream.

The incredible experience left Lenny wanting more, so he returned shortly after to repeat his ton-up-man-ship, leaving him feeling he would be having some amazing dreams for many nights to come. Now who was king of the road?

§

Shortly after his superbike had lived up to its name, Maggie asked Lenny to take her to the Paris Cinema in Coventry to see *To Sir with Love*. She attended grammar school and was interested in the contrasting fortunes of pupils from the tough inner-city London school depicted in the film. It starred the brilliant Sidney Poitier and the title track was sung by Lulu. Lenny agreed on the spur of the moment and Maggie got herself dolled up in double-quick time. They were running slightly late to catch the evening matinee, but Lenny knew how to sort that. Accelerating over Gibbet Hill with the straight mile ahead, Lenny let rip right up to the ton, in racing mode with Maggie in tandem, but the traffic lights were on red and it required skill to pull up in time.

Fortunately, Lenny was now accomplished at this and knew exactly how to slow safely: decelerating through the gears to avoid locking up the back wheel; sitting bolt upright to use the body as a drag chute; and tickling the brakes to a stop. At the lights, Lenny looked round to check if Maggie was okay and found the ton had not been without consequence – her beautiful hair now resembled a bale of tumbleweed from a spaghetti western and her eye make-up had run across her face. When the lights changed, they continued on to the Paris Cinema, not exceeding the city speed limit and, after Maggie had tidied herself up, they thoroughly enjoyed the film, thinking it worth the rush.

Maggie was keen to watch her boyfriend play football, so he agreed to bring her over to a pre-season friendly one warm July evening. Usually, Lenny wasn't that keen on pre-season matches as they meant rock-hard pitches and dry throats, but this one he would never forget-straight after the game he took Maggie over to the social club to get a drink, and while they were there, they joined the crowd glued to the television watching the Apollo 11 Moon landing.

§

Dad's good friend, Harry King, was in the process of forming a new football team, but what made this one different was the fact that their games were to be played on Sundays. This had been given the green light by the Church, which had previously objected as it was The Day of Rest, but had now changed its tune and come on song.

Harry wanted Lenny to play centre forward for his team, which boasted a couple of ex-professionals along with a talented squad and, as it would not interfere with his Saturday football commitment to play for the works' side, Lenny agreed.

For Dad, Saturday usually meant doing an overtime shift in the morning, then watching Coventry City play in the afternoon as he was a season ticket holder. Dad felt great pride in his son's recent achievements and now that Lenny played on Sundays he often showed up to watch. One match, shortly after Lenny started, Dad was standing over by the corner flag close to the action when Lenny accidentally collided with an opponent. The player leapt up, red mist descending, and lashed out with both fists. Lenny felt adequately protected by his own straight left, which Dad had taught him, combined with the Ali Shuffle in defence, but his dad brought matters to a speedy conclusion, pulling out the corner flag and bopping the player on the head to bring the affray to an abrupt end. Dad replaced the flag with everybody on the line saying it was fair dos. Lenny felt he to be the aggrieved party, so it was shrugged shoulders with open palms, and the ref agreed, awarding him a free kick.

# Testing Times

Dad's biggest fear, apart from Lenny killing himself on the road, was that his son might pack up his apprenticeship midway to take up a precarious football career. Much that Dad loved football, he thought it should wait until Lenny had completed his apprenticeship so the boy would have something to fall back on. Although Lenny had not received any definite offers, his uncle repeated that he would be welcome at Middlesbrough, where Lenny's cousin Gordon Jones was captain, but it seemed a long way from home and Middlesbrough was not a fashionable club. Nevertheless, Dad thought it was worth talking up recent changes to the five-year apprenticeship scheme that by now, due to an agreement between the government and trade unions, had been reduced to four. Dad really talked this up, hoping to strike a chord and get Lenny to stay, but his trump card was always Maggie, who had no intentions of letting Lenny go anywhere unless she accompanied him.

For the time being though, the only place Lenny was going was Butlins – Maggie had spotted an all-inclusive holiday package for two in the Sunday newspaper and the holiday camp in North Wales seemed most affordable.

Pwllheli was quite a ride and the couple clocked up over 150 miles on the journey. On arrival the motorbike was locked in a secure pound and they were given the keys to a brightly painted chalet with single bunks. The couple enjoyed their five-night break away, especially the Butlins' cable car, which afforded great views of the bay. On the day they were due to return, the weather was lovely and Lenny cruised at around 80mph through the amazing Snowdonia National Park in the sunshine, his beautiful Maggie snuggly tucked in behind, the perfect pillion passenger – at one with bike and rider. All along the route, admirers stopped to watch and wave as the pair thundered by. This is it, Lenny thought, there is nothing better – he truly was king of the road – and he waved back, revelling in the attention. But, just after Ffestiniog, dazzled by all the adulation and the sunshine's glare, Lenny turned back from waving to see a blind tunnel appearing from nowhere – unable to see the light at the end and fearing that they were heading straight for a wall of death, Maggie intuitively leant away, something she had never done before, and Lenny came round, realised it was a dog-leg, and desperately banked hard to the right.

The surface, the camber, the tyres, the forks, all held for that moment in that dark tunnel waiting for deliverance. The bike held, took the dog-leg and shot towards the bright light now visible at the end. Sweating with fear, heart thudding against his ribs, Lenny straightened the bike and rode it out of the tunnel into the sunshine. He didn't stop to check on Maggie. He didn't stop to calm his nerves. He continued – though at a slower speed – keeping his terror inside, not wanting to admit to himself or his girlfriend that he had nearly caused their demise.

Back in Kenilworth, the shell-shocked lad dropped his girlfriend home and went back to his house. He garaged the bike and went straight to his room. That night he couldn't stop the incident from replaying in his mind as he lay there in the dark. Every time he closed his eyes, he saw the darkness of the tunnel and his heart started pounding again. Maggie, too, he knew had been troubled – when she dismounted she had not said a word about the near fatality – and he wondered if she would ever trust him enough to ride pillion again.

§

Lenny and Maggie weren't the only ones experiencing a change of heart about fast bikes. After an accident one evening on the bend in Ashow, which sent Jim to hospital, Jim's dad hatched a plan to rid his son of that dangerous form of transport and replace it with a car. The deal he proposed was that he would get Jim a Mini and help him pass his test if, when the bike was repaired, Jim would sell it.

Jim went for it. He passed his driving test and became the proud owner of a little green Mini, all within two months. When the car arrived, the whole chapter went round to Jim's house to look it over. It wasn't a bike, but they liked it, and they all took turns sitting in the driver's seat while tooting the horn. Then they all had a laugh trying to squeeze everyone in the back.

Keen to try out his little green Mini, Jim suggested a weekend away in Lenny's little green tent. Having been away together on a school trip to Snowdonia where they conquered Tryfan, Jim wanted to go one step further and conquer Snowdon, adding a twist he had read about in a climbing magazine. The idea was to climb to the top of the mountain, then jump off, sliding back down on the mountain scree – a real buzz for thrill seekers. Lenny thought doing the ton was a safer option, but agreed to give it a go.

§

Straightaway the Mini exceeded expectations by comfortably holding the luggage with room to spare. Then it was off up the A5, cruising at a steady 60mph, with Lenny seriously starting to rethink his motoring future; although for him a car would be a big step up financially.

After about three hours, the lads found themselves at the head of Llanberis Pass. They made their way halfway down and set up camp at the foot of Snowdon. Having secured a good pitch, they set up the primus for a hot meal of spam, beans and egg, washed down with a big mug of tea. The plan was to set off straight after breakfast the following day and climb up the side of Snowdon to the massive scree slope, then jump on it and slide all the way to the bottom. All they needed was their climbing boots and a pair of leather gloves according to the magazine. The technique, it said, was to sit on one boot with the other straight out and use the hands either side as stabilisers; but on no account, the article warned, should they lean forward else the climber could tumble out of control.

The next morning, they stuck to their plan. They took a couple of test jumps on a lower slope to hone the technique then ascended above the scree line and found a safe place to leap from. Jim launched himself first, and it worked: he glided down and down and down to the bottom of the scree slope at the foot of Snowdon. Then he turned and waved at Lenny for his turn, the lad following with equal success. Having spent a long day on the mountain, it was back to camp for a well-earned mug of tea and some beans.

The lads had intended to stay another night and return home on the Sunday morning, but having achieved their objective and with the weather on the turn, they felt there was little point hanging about, and if they got a move on, they would get back in time for the disco that night at the Crackley Tennis Club. So they broke camp, stuffed everything back in the Mini and set off, keeping an eye out for a chip shop on the way.

In the rush to return, Jim pushed the little green Mini to its limits, and Lenny was impressed at how it handled: responding well, and when it came to roundabouts having the engine at the front along with the drive made it stick like glue. Jim also found he could throw the Mini into a bend and drive through at speed, which was not possible on a motorbike and turned out to be quite a thrill – almost as appealing as jumping off mountains and doing the ton.

The lads made it to the disco in time, only to find it was all ticket, but they managed to bluff their way in for the last dance – the dark disguising their climbing boots and the lads being careful not to tread on any toes.

Reflecting back on the weekend, Lenny decided he liked the Mini's ability to protect him from the elements. And there was the space for carrying both luggage and passengers in the car's favour too. Though he didn't admit it to himself at the time, he was also relieved that the return from Snowdonia had been free from incident. Just one Mini-break away had planted a seed in Lenny's mind.

# Mini Van

A decent Mini car could cost hundreds of pounds, which Lenny simply did not have. But in the commercial section of the classified advertisements in the Coventry Evening Telegraph, Lenny spotted a Mini van for sale: spares or repairs, drives well, twenty pounds. The van was at a farm just a couple of fields away so he thought it would be worth a ramble. When he arrived, the farmer told him he could take it for a test drive, but Lenny didn't really know how to drive so when, a few hundred yards along the lane, it conked out he had to go back to get the farmer, who came along and simply pushed the choke back in. For twenty pounds Lenny thought he couldn't go wrong, so he bought the van and drove it home. It might not be a Mini *car*, but it had exactly the same front end and a longer wheelbase, which would make it even better round bends.

The little blue Mini van drove well. But it didn't stop well. The brakes were a bit spongy due to air in the system, but the farmer thought they probably just needed bleeding. It had quite a long MOT, which meant it could go straight on the road as soon as Lenny had bought tax, but it was a bit of a rot-box. Also some urgent repairs were required as the passenger seat was pushing through the well. This was no problem to a fixer like Lenny, and he bought some sheet metal and pop rivets to strengthen it up. Then, the following morning, it was back to Jack Parker's for a cover note and over to the Warwick tax office to get a disc. The van was now legal. All that was required was for the driver to be too.

The test date came with just a month to prepare and, right up to the day, Lenny was out practising: reversing, parking, hill starts. But the van's brakes were not getting any better and they needing pumping – pushing the pedal up and down quickly – to get the van to stop. With all the driving practice, Lenny had not paid much attention to his Highway Code and had left this to the last minute to thumb through.

On the big day things did not get off to a good start. The examiner opened the passenger door and it fell off. Lenny had to explain that it wasn't used very often. Also the examiner was a big man – made bigger by wearing a thick coat that filled the passenger well – and Lenny hoped the floor would be strong enough to hold for the duration of the test.

Once the examiner had reattached the door, he issued his instructions and Lenny drove off. The lad felt confident, but was a little concerned about his ability to emergency stop as the brakes didn't work unless the pedal was frequently pumped. Fortunately, the examiner could not see what was going on down at the pedals, where some nifty footwork was occurring. And it was a good job the van had a horn as, halfway up Campion Hill, a dog decided to walk out into the middle of the road. Lenny wasn't quite sure what to do, so he slowed down and tooted the dog until it moved over. This seemed to satisfy the examiner, and once the boy had performed his emergency stop satisfactorily, the big man gave instructions to pull up outside the test centre where he introduced the Highway Code. This was a struggle and Lenny did not know whether he was getting his answers right or wrong, but his sixth sense detected the examiner was trying to help him by producing a couple of easy questions to conclude the test.

'I am sorry to tell you, Mr Unsworth,' the examiner said when they had finished, 'that you almost failed your test on the Highway Code.'

Lenny looked down at the wheel.

'Does that mean I've passed?' he asked.

The examiner nodded. 'Yes, son. Now let me out of this rust bucket before I fall through the floor.'

Lenny couldn't have been more excited to get his pink slip, and that evening when Dad enquired who had accompanied him on his drive to the test centre, he simply waved the pink slip at his father and smiled.

In truth, Dad wasn't bothered. He was just relieved his son would now be safe; he couldn't wait to see the back of 'that' motorbike and he locked it up in the shed so it couldn't be used.

§

John's Yamaha soon made it three Chapter motorbikes off the road, awaiting parts from Japan, which didn't look like they would be arriving anytime soon, but the lads had fun looking at his carburettor on the mantelpiece. That only left Gordon, who shortly afterwards got himself a three-wheeler. Virtually overnight the motorbike chapter had disbanded into an auto club and the parents breathed a collective sigh of relief.

§

Lenny's top priority was to get the Mini van roadworthy. Jim had just taken up an apprenticeship with Kenilworth Car Bodies, learning all about welding, while Lenny had covered the skill during his first year of training. The lads had an idea to get hold of some oxyacetylene bottles so they could weld up the Mini van and then make a bit of money on the side doing repairs for other people. They drove over to Terry Road in Coventry, where the British Oxygen Company had a depot, signed the necessary forms and came back with a set of bottles. Dad let the lads set up a workshop in his garage, and it soon became a hub for repairs, with Lenny's van being the first to get welded. That just left the brakes, which as the farmer said, needed bleeding.

Although it could not be denied that spinning wheels took place, economy soon became the new buzzword, and this signalled a complete U-turn on driving through bends at speed as well as a general lowering of the speed in order to achieve maximum miles per gallon. The motorbike days were well and truly over, but for Lenny, saying farewell to his Constellation friend did not come easy, even though the thirty pounds he sold it for came in useful.

# Rita

Having the car comforts of a heater combined with a van's access and space, Lenny had acquired a very versatile and economical motor and Dad was quick to pick up on this by ordering a load of paving slabs for collection by the little blue van. Also the lads realised there was money to be made welding and decided to offer a mobile sill-replacement service, which could arrive with all the necessary equipment in the back to undertake the task. They called themselves J & L Chassis Repairs, and local artist Alan Harwood agreed to sign-write this for them on the side of the van.

The morning after Lenny's nineteenth birthday, while tyre-kicking around his van as Alan set up to sign-write, Lenny couldn't help notice a lot of police activity going on in Dudley Road. Later that morning, news filtered through that a girl had gone missing the previous night. The girl turned out to be Rita Sawyer, an old classmate of Lenny's from Kenilworth School and the sister of one of his work colleagues, and Lenny had always been minded to sing the Beatles song "Lovely Rita" to her whenever he saw her. When Alan signed off, the lads went over to a local pub called the Kings Arms and all the talk there was of missing Rita too.

On the following Monday, driving his usual route to work past Warwick Castle and up Gallows Hill, Lenny saw a police roadblock diverting all the traffic. When he got into work, he heard the news that a girl's body had been found in a gateway on Harbury Lane. She had been brutally murdered. It was Rita.

The following police investigation questioned thousands of men but the murder remained unsolved for decades to come. After the police cordon had been lifted, Lenny visited the gateway where Rita had been found to silently pay his respects while wondering how this could have been.

# Old Friend

With the floor fixed, the door secure on its hinges and the brakes rid of air, the Mini van became a great little motor and Lenny grew to love it. He guessed that Maggie preferred it too – her make-up stayed in place, her hairstyles were protected from the wind and Lenny drove at a sensible pace, there being no possibility that the little blue van could do the ton. When a bike roared past, tank flashing in the sunshine, rider bent over the handlebars getting a thrill from the speed, Lenny still felt a pang of loss, but he was well and truly converted to cars and had no real desire to go back.

*Pic 14, Learner driver Ben, pointing out Alans artwork*

Now being a qualified driver, along with his own set of wheels made Lenny most popular amongst an old gang of school friends. Lenny agreed to help one with some driving lessons, while also agreeing to take the gang for a September break to the foothills of Snowdonia. This was to be a camp-over, but Lenny didn't need a tent on this occasion. His plan was to sleep in the van, proving once again its versatility, before returning everybody safely back home.

During the final year of his apprenticeship, Lenny found himself placed in an engineering workshop abbreviated to MTR – machine tool reconditioning – where he found the work really interesting. He started to talk about making a career out of it, which Dad welcomed, while talk about a football trial with Stoke City he did not. Most evenings Lenny went round to Maggie's house, but if he didn't call, it would not set off any alarm bells. Things had settled down for Lenny, he was happy and life was good.

Then one evening, an old friend from way back came round, boasting about his dad's brand new Hillman Imp. The friend's handle was Flat Out, which was his style, and he was keen to demonstrate the rear-engine, rear-wheel-drive features of the Imp; features that made it notoriously light at the front end while not affecting the acceleration.

Off into the countryside they sped, calling at a pub called the Stags Head for a couple of pints before heading home along Offchurch Lane. Flat Out knew the lane well and picked up speed on the descent as they approached the humpback bridge that spanned the canal at the bottom. When they reached the foot of the hill, Flat Out accelerated, causing the front end to lift off from the crown of the bridge when they hit it. The car thudded back down noisily on the other side, producing a fairground-like thrill for the lads inside. It was so good that Flat Out decided to go back up the hill and repeat it. Lenny's days of dangerous thrill-seeking were over, however. He told Flat Out to pack it up, but this only seemed to spur his friend on. Ignoring Lenny's protest, Flat Out screeched the Imp back up to the top of the hill, turned it, let off the brake, and – whooping – let the car fly down the hill again. When it reached the bottom, Flat Out rammed the accelerator to the floor and this time it wasn't two wheels that left the road, it was all four. The Imp took off, sailing through the air before smashing back down on to the road, crashing through a fence, and hurtling out of control towards a huge oak tree, which it hit head-on.

The Imp lay a mangled mess on the side of the canal, and Lenny lay trapped inside, bleeding heavily from his head. This time, he thought, as he slipped in and out of consciousness, my run of lucky escapes is over. But his friend wasn't about to give up on him; he scrambled out of the wreckage and ran flat out in the direction of the lock-keeper's cottage he could see down the lane. He needed to get help. He needed to get to a phone.

For Lenny the clock was ticking. He tried in vain to pull himself free from the wreckage. The Imp was a time bomb. Petrol everywhere. One spark from the ignition and the whole scene would go up in a fireball. Meanwhile, Flat Out had reached the cottage and was panting out what had happened. Soon sirens filled the air, and the police, fire and ambulance services combined to provide the necessary response.

A fire watch was set up to stand guard while the firefighters cut Lenny free. The ambulance crew applied emergency dressings to stem the flow of blood from his head. Throughout all, Lenny remained conscious and only slipped into unconsciousness once he was freed and in the ambulance, racing to Warwick A&E with a high-speed police escort, perfect teamwork providing the lad with a chance.

# No Mirrors

Dad arrived at the hospital to be told Lenny was unconscious and had three serious head injuries for which he had received thirty-eight stitches. Dad could not believe that after all he'd been through his son lay close to death as a car passenger. Surgeons had been put on standby as there was evidence of a possible skull depression, which could mean internal bleeding, and Dad was required to sign forms giving consent to operate should his son's condition deteriorate.

Early in the morning on his second day in hospital, Lenny regained a low level of consciousness. Lying on his back, he knew where he was and why he was there. He did not know however, the extent of his injuries, so he decided to give himself a medical. Starting at the bottom, he wiggled his toes, then he stretched his arms up and touched his nose, but when he tried to lift his legs, he was met by a sharp pain in his lower back. The nurse spotted him moving and came over to attend.

'We nearly lost you,' she said. 'How are you feeling?'

Lenny indicated he was suffering back pain, so she rolled him on to his side and lifted his smock to investigate, discovering shards of glass embedded in his back. After all the glass had been removed, Lenny lay flat again and closed his eyes; he was relieved to be alive, and grateful to be in the expert hands of the Warwick Hospital staff once more.

Five days after being admitted in a comatose state, the visible effects were obvious, although not for Lenny as he wasn't allowed a mirror. He could now receive visitors, but not anyone under eighteen, so the matron arranged for Lenny to wave out of the window to Maggie and little Julie. Mum cried on seeing her son in such a battered and bruised state, and cried again when the doctors told her Lenny had suffered nerve damage to the left side of his face and could expect to experience dizziness, which would need close monitoring, meaning he would have to stay in hospital for at least another week.

Having taken thirty-eight without complaint, removal of all the bonded-in, dried-blood stitches received thirty-eight complaints, but this was a good sign and indicated things were on the mend. Nevertheless, there was a long way to go and the doctors warned of post-concussion syndrome, which could include memory problems, sickness, tiredness and depression. Plenty of rest with care was their prescription, along with a warning that any blow to the head could be fatal – Lenny was not to even think about football.

Now the lad was on the mend, his bed was moved away from the nurse station and set up alongside the ward's wag, who cheerfully told him this was a good sign – the criticals were always kept up by the exit for easy access to the morgue with minimal ward disruption. He added that Lenny's arrival had caused quite a stir by the additional service of two nuns, who had stayed with him during his hours of need with their Rosary prayers. These guardian angels visited the ward daily and Lenny found them most comforting, as did Dad, who during Lenny's darkest hours had prayed with them over his son.

The afternoon of Lenny's second week in hospital, a familiar face appeared carrying a punnet of the fattest, blackest grapes imaginable. It took Lenny a few moments to recognise the bearer because he was not wearing his cow-gown. Bearing gifts of fruit, along with a card signed by all the staff at Burgis and Colbourne, Albert conveyed Lenny get-well wishes. The lad wondered how they knew about his accident, but Albert told him 'bad news travels fast' and that they were expecting a visit when he got out of hospital. Shaking hands with his old boss, Lenny readily agreed.

§

After two weeks, having said his goodbyes and with all the paperwork in place, it was time for Lenny to be discharged. Instructions were to have as much rest as possible and avoid any exertion. He was signed off work for a further month and told to return straight back to hospital in the event of any dizzy spells. There was to be no driving, and football was cancelled for the foreseeable future. All this was a lot to take in, but the last instruction seemed the hardest to swallow.

That said, it felt great to be back home amongst his family. Little sister Julie, having been scared by the visit to see her brother in hospital, was now comfortable to examine his scars with childlike inquisition and even Blackie got a lick! Although one special person was missing, but Mum said she would be round after college. All day, Lenny clock-watched, eagerly anticipating Maggie's arrival, planning what he was going to say. When she finally arrived and they got a moment in private, they lovingly embraced. There might even have been mention of a ring.

# Managing Expectations

Now that Lenny was on the mend, the top priority was to get him back to work as soon as possible. Dad had already been in contact with the Lockheed and they said that an early return would be favourable to avoid any retakes, but that his job was secure, and this came as a relief.

As for the driver of the Imp and repentant source of Lenny's circumstances, he waited until Lenny's dad's Beetle was off the drive and then went round to see how things were going. The news was that the police were going to interview everybody involved. They suspected thrill seekers and they wanted to press charges of reckless driving, which could carry a custodial sentence. There had been a report from the lock-keeper's cottage that *two* heavy thuds had been heard on the night of the accident, so any talk from Lenny about going back up to the top of the hill to come back down again would have serious implications. Additionally, the written-off Imp was a company car and Flat Out's dad's job was in jeopardy. When the police interviewed Lenny, they drily suggested that the Grand Old Duke of York had been in the area, but Lenny just gave an account of what he could remember at the time, and as he was suffering from amnesia, which is common to head trauma, he could only remember descending the hill once. When pressed for an explanation of what could have caused two heavy thuds, Lenny offered the suggestion of a loose sluice. Once the interviews had concluded, Flat Out was charged with dangerous driving and laid at the mercy of the court, receiving three endorsements on his licence along with a heavy fine while the services received commendations, not least from Lenny.

§

After three weeks of hanging about the house counting his get-well cards, Lenny decided to break out on a cycle ride to Leamington Spa. It was quite a smooth ride, with Lenny finding he could balance reasonably well, only encountering one wobbly moment as he entered the town. Keeping to his word, he went to visit Albert, who said, while chatting over a cup of tea and a KitKat, that he was surprised to see the lad so soon. Together they went on a tour of the store so Lenny could thank as many of the staff as possible for their kind wishes. Then Lenny pedalled back to Kenilworth, this time keeping to the pavement for a safe return.

When the date came for Lenny's final appointment, the specialist said he was prepared to sign his patient off to return to work on the condition that there would be no heavy lifting. Also, Lenny would be able to get back behind the wheel, which was great news. Contact sports – including football – were completely ruled out though, and this left Lenny gutted, despite suggestions of darts and table tennis to improve hand-eye coordination.

Returning to work, Lenny was placed under the stewardship of Ernie Shepherd on a lathe section of the MTR, as this was considered light duties. Although Lenny had been off work for a while, it didn't feel like he had missed much and by now he was well into his final year of training. The ideal situation for an apprentice in this last year was to get into a suitable department that might have a future for him and then be offered a job by the section manager. Lenny was lucky enough to achieve this and Dad could not have been more delighted. Lenny was pleased too, but his acceptance of the appointment appeared to hammer the final nail in the coffin of his football dreams.

*Pic 15, Saturday afternoon action on Parliament Piece.*

*Pic 16, Team transport*

But dreams it seems, like Beetles and dogs, can be resurrected, and a few weeks later Eric Teale, the Saint Nicholas Boys' Club leader, who had recently taken up employment in the Lockheed's tool room, popped through to see how Lenny was. On hearing the disappointed lad lament his beloved game, Eric came up with an option.

'Why not coach a Boys' Club team?' he suggested, telling Lenny he would handle the paperwork if Lenny would manage the team.

Enthusiastically, Lenny accepted and stepped up to the challenge of becoming the team manager for these U16s; and the little blue van rose to the challenge too, providing transport for the whole team to Saturday afternoon away fixtures – although not comfortably, but this was a price his passengers were willing to pay.

# Post Script

To all the Eric's of this world who give up their free time for the benefit of others. Thank you. Thank you. Thank you. That said, Lenny made a good recovery from his accident, and despite his fears of never playing football again, debuted for Stoneleigh FC the day after his twentieth birthday on September 5th 1971. Twenty-seven years later he played his 500th game before going on to manage and coach various local sides. In 2014, he played what could possibly be his last match against his own son in a dads v lads competition at Kenilworth School, Leyes Lane.

# About the Author

Len Unsworth was born in Coventry and grew up in Kenilworth, where he has spent the majority of his adult life. Now retired, Len devotes most of his time to caring for his two beautiful children, taking them to and from school and their many after-school activities. Through them and their joy of learning, he has been able to reminisce about some of his own childhood experiences. *Kenilworth Chapter* is his second memoir; its predecessor *Educating Kenilworth* follows a younger Lenny through his tumultuous years at St Nicholas and Kenilworth schools.